Martha Gellhorn:
Myth, Motif
and Remembrance

Angelia H. Dorman

Thanks for shopping with us.
Kindest Regards, Customer Care

RETURNING GOODS

Please re-pack, in the original packaging if possible, and send back to us at the address below. **Caution!** Don't cover up the barcode (on original packaging) as it helps us to process your return.

We will email you when we have processed your return.

---✂--

PLEASE complete and include this section with your goods.

Your Name: _____

Your Order Number _____

Reason for return _____

Select: Refund my order ☐   **Replace my order** ☐

(Please note, if we are unable to replace the item it will be refunded.)

Return to:

---✂--

```
RETURNS
Unit 22, Horcott Industrial Estate
Horcott Road
FAIRFORD
GL7 4BX
```

FOR MY FAMILY

David, Sarah and James

CONTENTS

ACKNOWLEDGMENTS

Dr. Jacqueline Orsagh was the first person to examine the life and work of Martha Gellhorn. All other work on Gellhorn is built upon her original manuscript *A Critical Biography of Martha Gellhorn*. It was written before the digital revolution, when research was done by hand in archives and manuscripts were written on typewriters, and it remains the taproot of all Gellhorn scholarship. I am much obliged to her for her kindness, input, patience and time. I am also grateful for her support, and most of all her continued friendship.

Successful research is dependent on archival work. My thanks go to the many librarians and archivists who have been patient with me and generous with their time and energy. I was privileged to work with the late John Taylor, archivist at the National Archives. Mr. Taylor guided me through the Supreme Headquarters Allied Expeditionary Forces (SHAEF) materials and also made introductions to individuals who have been crucial to this study, most importantly Elizabeth (Betty) McIntosh. Her experience as a journalist, White House correspondent covering Mrs. Roosevelt, and as a member of the OSS in China helped keep me grounded in the era. She was also a sounding board for ideas and provided encouragement throughout this process. Milt Wolff provided me with a regular place to stay in the Bay Area, crucial background information, and explicit details which added to my understanding of events and specific portions of Gellhorn's life. He provided criticism on certain portions of this work, always reminded me to keep my sense of humor on this journey.

The basis of this book is my doctoral dissertation. I was given a piece of good advice early and that was to choose an advisor and dissertation director wisely. It was the best advice I could have ever been given and I followed it. I owe a tremendous debt of gratitude to Dr. Pingchao Zhu of the History Department at the University of Idaho. She has not only been my advisor, she has been a guide, friend and mentor throughout this endeavor. Her support and criticism and got me through the most difficult parts of this process. She truly is the best! I am also very grateful for the time and energy and input by my other committee members. I am especially appreciative of Dr. Dale Graden who guided me through a whole phase of the development of my understanding of Latin America, Dr. Anna Banks challenged me to see the world through the lens of film and that added a new dynamic to the way I understand the influence of popular culture on history, and Dr. Ian Chambers brought a fresh perspective to this process. Also, my thanks to Cheri Cole at the University of Idaho Graduate School for her patience and assistance.

For their early and continuing support, my thanks go to Dr. Marcia Synnott, the late Dr. Owen Connelly and the late Dr. H. Henry Lumpkin of the University of South Carolina, Dr. Reina Pennington of Norwich University and Dr. Rich Crane of Greensboro College. Dr. Gary Hoff provided a critical travel grant which allowed me to meet with Martha Gellhorn the first time, which led to subsequent visits. Also, thanks to Barry and Celia Fogden, Alison Classe, Virginia Weathers, Jo Cottingham, Monica Martinez and Shawn Colvin. As always, my Mom, Dad and Granny gave me their constant support.

Finally, I owe a deep and tremendous debt of gratitude to Martha Gellhorn. Martha was kind enough to answer my letters and correspond with me for the last ten years of her life. She was gracious enough to allow me to visit her in her London flat both in 1991 and in 1995. She was patient enough to read portions of what I had written about her and kind with her criticisms.

None of this could have been accomplished without the support of my husband, David Dorman, who has had to live with both me and Martha Gellhorn through this process.

INTRODUCTION

Martha Gellhorn was one of the most accomplished journalists of the 20th century. She left home at 21 setting off to become a foreign correspondent, and she did. Gellhorn covered wars and peace and chronicled a large part of the century. No matter how great her accomplishments, her eight year relationship with Ernest Hemingway largely dominates the way Gellhorn is remembered. His name was like a rock chained around her neck. However, in the final twenty years of her life she emerged from Hemingway's shadow. It is during that renaissance period, fifty years after she embarked on her youthful journey to become a novelist and foreign correspondent, that she reclaimed her accomplishments and the modern remembrance of Martha Gellhorn begins.

Martha Gellhorn's life began in St. Louis and was deeply rooted in her Progressive middle class upbringing. Raised in the insularity of an upper middle class free-thinking home, her standards were high and her world view was narrowly and clearly defined, early on. She expected the same attitude in others, applied it to the world and demanded it in return. When individuals or the world did not reciprocate, she did not tolerate it. Her vision was one born in the idealism of the Progressives Movement and lived in the complexities and constraints of the 20th Century.

She first fled St. Louis and then the United States as soon as she was old enough and her life as an expatriate began. As a young adult, she rejected St. Louis as stifling, saying she had learned as much as she could from St. Louis and moved on. She said the same of Bryn Mawr, dropping out and moving on. This pattern echoed in nearly all of her relationships, personal and professional. When she had learned all she could, exhausted what was valuable or came to the end of what she could continue to contribute, she ended the relationship. Ultimately, when she could no longer see value in her life and felt she had come to the end of her ability to contribute to society, she ended her own life.[1]

Gellhorn's youthful goal had been to become a foreign correspondent. The Progressive environment she was raised in led her to fully accept and embrace the belief that journalism could make a difference and early on she began to cast herself in the role of a crusading journalist. In 1959, she published her seminal collection of war journalism, *The Face of War*. In it she wrote:

> When I was young I believed in the perfectibility of man, and in progress, and thought of journalism as a guiding light. If people were told the truth, if dishonor and injustice were clearly shown to them, they would at once demand the saving action, punishment of wrong-doers, and care for the innocent…It took nine years, and a great depression and two wars ending in defeat, and one surrender without war to break my faith in the benign power of the press.[2]

Her route to becoming a foreign correspondent was not immediate, nor was it a direct course. When she arrived in Paris in 1930, she bounced around the continent writing primarily for her hometown newspaper *The St. Louis Post Dispatch*. She wrote a miserable failure of a novel and returned home to work as an investigator at large for the Federal Emergency Relief Administration (FERA). After leaving the FERA, she wrote a book about the Depression published in 1936. In 1937, she wound up in the midst of the civil war in Spain and by happenstance became a war correspondent. It was a seven year journey. In another seven years, she reached the pinnacle of her career as a war correspondent in the closing years of World War II.

Gellhorn openly rejected feminism, but is a role model to feminists. She was at the war front ahead of and in spite of her male competition. She was the self-made woman whose own accomplishments were overshadowed by her high profile brief marriage to Ernest Hemingway. She was always her own woman. She further cemented herself with feminist by being the only one of Hemingway's four wives who left him.

As much as she criticized Hemingway and the "mythomania" which surrounded his life, she, too, fully succumbed to her own version of myth making.[3] By the time she reached the final twenty years of life, she had carefully cultivated a mythology of her life; a mythology of Martha Gellhorn emerged.

Priding herself on her independence and her self-willed life, she traded on her looks and class connections. Her mother's friendship through the League of Women's Voters with Eleanor Roosevelt allowed Martha early and easy entree to Mrs. Roosevelt with whom she cultivated a genuine, strong, life-long relationship. This gave young Martha almost unparalleled access to the White House, as both visitor and regular correspondent of Eleanor Roosevelt with direct access to President Franklin Delano Roosevelt (FDR). She was never a journalist merely writing for the masses. Before she had written anything of substance, whether journalism or fiction, she was sending her comments and observations directly to the Roosevelts for their review. The Roosevelts are just one example of Gellhorn's privileged circle. While her power relationships were genuine friendships, it is still clear that she aimed for and attempted to influence an audience with political power, not just the mass market readers who read her published work.

Gellhorn fancied herself as a romantic writer in the mold of the Lost Generation. But, in all reality, her actions, subjects and career as reporter was more deeply rooted in the philosophy of Progressive journalism in the muckraker tradition. The path she took as a writer in the 20th Century reflected the ideals, complexity, shortcomings and limitations of her Progressive upbringing. Early on, Gellhorn seized upon the motifs in her writing and they formed the core values found in all of her work. Her commitment was to inform, educate and influence change.

In fiction, she drew a bigger picture and took greater liberty with events, using time, place and characters to illuminate the reader, allowing them to see for themselves life as she saw it in a more dramatic light. She succeeded two times in translating the muckraker pattern of realist journalism to realist novel. *The Trouble I've Seen* was her exposé of conditions during the Depression, and *A Stricken Field* attempted to educate readers regarding the Czech crisis of 1938. She was the researching, roving inquisitor, the journalist who took her talents to the next level as novelist and attempted to expose her readers to a broader deeper truth than journalism allowed. Sometimes she had success, other times she failed.

In the 1930s, she was youthful Marty to everyone. After World War II, she became permanently Martha. Young Marty Gellhorn's life reads like a brisk Hollywood movie script written for a slightly grittier Katherine Hepburn. All the while, she was developing the more mature, cool persona of "Martha Gellhorn" that she would eventually latch hold of and continue to mold. In the latter half of her life, she continued to transform that early image into a cooler more mature Lauren Bacall archetype, which she encouraged. She carefully cultivated the building blocks of that persona from the young crusading girl reporter image, to the pioneering woman war correspondent to the sage high empress of an influential group of younger well established writers who still today vehemently protect her image. Ultimately, she branded her image as "Martha Gellhorn."

Gellhorn's impulse to control her image was so strong that she attempted to control it even in death, closing her papers for 25 years after her death. That, like so many things pertaining to Gellhorn, had its exception also in the form of her official biographer, Carolyn Moorehead. Moorehead was handpicked by the estate and given exclusive access to the papers closed until 2023.[4]

Scholarship on Gellhorn vacillates between focusing on her personal life and career. It has shifted between works with a primary focus on Hemingway or a primary look at Gellhorn. Carlos Baker's *Ernest Hemingway: A Life Story* is the first biographical portrait of Gellhorn. It is narrow in its focus and deals primarily with Gellhorn's years with Hemingway, and it is biased toward Hemingway's version of his life with Gellhorn. Gellhorn comes across in *Ernest Hemingway: A Life Story* as a bitchy, bitter, social climber who uses Hemingway to advance her own career. While Baker received some input from Gellhorn, as with most situations dealing with Hemingway, she became frustrated in the process and stopped her exchange with Baker.[5] Gellhorn ran hot and cold on her life with Hemingway. He was unavoidable, in addition to being the great novelist of his time, she was romantically linked with him as lover and later as wife from the period of 1937-1945, her most productive period as a writer.

In the mid-1970s, Jacqueline Elizabeth Orsagh undertook the first critical biography of Gellhorn focusing on Gellhorn's literary legacy. Orsagh did extensive research and corresponded with Gellhorn, and eventually went to London to interview her. While Gellhorn was quite kind to her, Orsagh met with the same hot and cold extremism from Gellhorn. It was a pattern Gellhorn demonstrated time and again toward others delving in to her life, attempting to sift the facts from the myths and mistruths. Yes, Orsagh could bring a tape recorder, no she could not. However, Orsagh was privy to Gellhorn's scrapbooks and Gellhorn's on-the-record and off-the-record comments. When she transcribed her notes and sent them to Gellhorn, Gellhorn was livid.

It was not an issue as to accuracy. Orsagh was accurate and attempted to double check that accuracy with Gellhorn, but there were too many personal comments written down for Gellhorn's taste. In Gellhorn's reporting, specifics and context are crucial, but she did not extend that to details regarding her own life.[6] Eventually, Gellhorn read Orsagh's dissertation in the fall of 1989 and made notations and corrections. What is most noteworthy in that document are the choices Gellhorn made correcting Orsagh; when and what she chose to add as commentary in this unpublished revision of her life gives a glimpse of Gellhorn as the editor of her own narrative. She had the opportunity to pick and choose what information to clarify. She had the opportunity to add commentary. The document is as much revealing regarding what she chose to comment upon in the biography, as what she chose to deliberately leave ambiguous.[7]

Bernice Kert's *The Hemingway Women* was the first mass-market Hemingway biography to have a major focus on Gellhorn.[8] It also marked the way Gellhorn would begin to be portrayed, as the accomplished war correspondent and not as Baker's leach. Kert follows Orsagh's dissertation very closely. Kert's biography used longer excerpts from Gellhorn's work and portions of Gellhorn and Hemingway's correspondence. In essence, it was an expanded version of Orsagh's work. The title alone incensed Gellhorn. However, Kert's book coincided with a renewed interest in

Gellhorn's life, separate from Hemingway. It also begins to establish Gellhorn firmly with feminists by bringing to the forefront the fact that of all of The *Hemingway Women*, she was the only one of his four wives who walked away from him.

Carl Rollyson's *Nothing Ever Happens to the Brave* was the first mass-market biography focusing solely on Gellhorn.[9] Rollyson's timing was excellent in that he was able to track down and interview a range of people from Gellhorn's childhood, college and early adult life. Due to their ages, many of them died in the years immediate following the publication of *Nothing Ever Happens to the Brave*. Again, as with Kert, Orsagh's work is borrowed upon heavily. The book was published in 1990 in spite of Gellhorn's attempts to block publication. She noted "all the long distance calls, faxes, lawyer, to say nothing of my page by page study for wrong facts and libels were pointless." [10] She was obsessed with stopping him, but unable. She did, however, force changes to Rollyson's original text. He published a second revised edition of the biography after Gellhorn's death. *Beautiful Exile: The Life of Martha Gellhorn* was an update of the original version. Rollyson described it as "a redline edition" of *Nothing Ever Happens to the Brave* including the details which he had been forced to omit in the earlier edition.[11]

Gellhorn was particularly appalled at Rollyson's account of her being married to Bertrand de Jouvenel.[12] The mistake on Rollyson's part was an honest one. Gellhorn's response was typical. She was aghast at the mistake, but did nothing to clarify the issue, nor did she take any responsibility for the mistake. Not all of his information was accurate, but he made an effort to keep his information as accurate as possible. Gellhorn would have had taken issue with anyone writing a biography of her, but she was particularly venomous when it came to Rollyson. There are flaws in Rollyson's interpretations of Gellhorn's letters and some of the facts he found are debatable. His final work was the most exhaustive look at Gellhorn's life until Caroline Moorehead's *Gellhorn: A Twentieth Century Life.*[13]

Moorehead is clear regarding the core aspects of Gellhorn's legacy. It was Gellhorn's voice and her ability to focus on people and the effect of war on people, not necessarily battles, which distinguishes her war reportage. Moorehead openly acknowledges that it is possible that reporting was moving in this direction all along and that Gellhorn was in the vanguard. Moorehead is correct. Gellhorn was not alone in this process. Lee Miller, Margaret Bourke-White and other war reporters both male and female were beginning to make those same shifts in focus from battlefield box score reportage to a more human portrait of the effects of war in their articles and photographs. Moorehead was a friend of Gellhorn's and the estate granted her almost exclusive access to Gellhorn's papers and personal letters.

Caroline Moorehead allowed Kate McLoughlin access to Gellhorn's letters and paper for her work, *Martha Gellhorn: The War Writer in the Field and in the Text.* McLoughlin's work is a deep textual analysis of Gellhorn's war writing. She juxtaposes Gellhorn's texts in their varying forms, comparing and contrasting them with broader ideas about war and war writing. While her focus is primarily on the position in the field and the relevant textual position of Gellhorn, she explores the varying versions of the war articles and how they fit a larger general picture of war reportage, and how Gellhorn's writing constructed a truth from the recollections of the battlefield, and how that fits a larger general picture. McLoughlin's close analysis of Gellhorn's editing of her own work begins to chip away at the façade of Gellhorn's mythology of war correspondent.[14] While McLoughlin concerns herself with place and text, she gives only cursory mention to Gellhorn in relation to other women in the field at the same time and in the same places producing similar work.

Moorehead edited and published *The Collected Letter's of Martha Gellhorn* in 2006. This volume does more to illuminate Gellhorn's life than any other single publication and it has not been utilized in any other major work to date. It is Gellhorn's most prolific outpouring and from it the reader gets a greater sense of the ebb and flow of her emotions and her commentary on her personal and professional life spanning 66 years. It is a taste of what is in store when the Martha Gellhorn Collection eventually opens in 2023.[15]

The core of the mythology of Martha Gellhorn is her collection of war reporting *The Face of War*. Originally published in 1959, with a late 1960s republication and a revised edition in 1988, the book is the taproot of Gellhorn's legacy. In the 1959 version of *The Face of War*, Gellhorn begins to shape her legacy as much by the articles she includes, as those she excludes. She clearly and intentionally placed each chosen piece of her war journalism included in the book and wrote a brief editorial introduction to each decade's work. While there were dozens of other articles she wrote as a war correspondent, Gellhorn's culling of the mundane is critical. It is from that carefully chosen core collection of Gellhorn's work and her commentary that Gellhorn began to frame the way she portrayed herself and the way she is remembered.[16] She further cements her image with a 1988 edition of *The Face of War* in which she includes her articles from Vietnam and Central America, and a volume of her non-war reporting and political commentary *The View from the Ground.*[17]

A cult of Gellhorn has emerged. Martha Gellhorn is portrayed in popular culture as "the first female war correspondent" which is highly inaccurate.[18] While Gellhorn and Marie Colvin are compared, there is very little mention or comparison of Gellhorn to the women who were writing and working as equals alongside Gellhorn.[19] Gellhorn was able to find her way to the front during the period from the Spanish Civil War through World War II, but she was not the only woman to do so, nor did she do it alone. An example of the perpetuation of this cult of Gellhorn is from Ward Just. Just touts Gellhorn as "the finest journalist in Vietnam," but she was in Vietnam for only several weeks.[20] There were other reporters in Saigon equally as outraged and other women actually on the front lines, like Dickie Chapelle who lost her life in the jungle on patrol with a Marine Corps unit.[21]

Building onto her published legacy, there is a cadre of journalists, writers, publisher friends, like John Pilger, John Snow, Bill Buford, John Simpson, Nicholas Shakespeare, and Ward Just, known in her circle as her "chaps." Their status and their overstatements of Gellhorn's historical position and have heavily influenced how Gellhorn is remembered.[22] They have warped Martha Gellhorn into something she was not, perpetuating a myth in print and film which overshadows by hyperbole and does an injustice to Gellhorn's actual accomplishments.[23]

BBC presenter and Gellhorn friend John Snow calls her "the greatest (war correspondent) that ever lived, bar none."[24] These over-the-top statements are incorrect and while I have no desire to disparage her accomplishments and contributions as a writer, foreign correspondent or liberal, I do believe that Gellhorn's legacy will benefit by settling her in to a more appropriate historical place. That place is some where between extremes.

Current scholarship has focused on esoteric textual analysis of Gellhorn's writing or has trended toward traditional longitudinal biography. These are contrasted with journalistic popular culture remembrances which overstate the narrative of Martha Gellhorn's life via a series of articles and media interviews where hyperbole drowns the subtlety and warmth of Gellhorn's voice.

Only summary analysis has been undertaken when discussing the influence of Gellhorn's family on her choice to become a journalist in the muckraker tradition. Her early ideals, in combination with her family values, cemented Gellhorn's lifelong mores and influenced her view of the role and social function of reporters and reporting, and directly affected the motifs found in her writing.

The publication of Carolyn Moorhead's collection of Gellhorn's letters only scratches the surface of this avenue of research. Quantities of important correspondence between Gellhorn and Eleanor Roosevelt, Edna Gellhorn and others were omitted from Moorehead's collection in favor of more personal selections. This study uses previously unpublished correspondence to flesh out my thesis especially in terms of her relationship with her family, her insecurity and ambivalence regarding a number of major life/career choices.

Previous work has avoided any focus on the areas where Gellhorn's thinking and observations are patently out of sync with modern or even late 20th century accepted norms. At times, Gellhorn's letters and writing show a paternalistic bend, with her ideas often bordering on social Darwinism and a call for eugenics. These observations are especially acute in her coverage of the Depression in America, in Asia and the Caribbean in *Collier's.*

In scholarship and discussion of Gellhorn, there has been a tendency to overlook the flaws in the mythology that grew up around Gellhorn during the last 20 years of her life. The caricature of Gellhorn as the fearless cocksure war correspondent is deeply flawed. Gellhorn was at times unsure, adrift in her life, during these times she often latched onto covering war. Her war "tourism" served as a distraction from personal issues and gave her a feeling of action and activism at times when she felt powerless to deal with larger issues. This is particularly evidenced in World War II and later with her brief trip to Vietnam, as well as her conscious decision not to cover the Korean War.

There is a large gap between Gellhorn's public persona as one who desired distance from mainstream Hemingway myths and in turn created her own Hemingway myth. She was the wife who stood up to him and walked out on him, something he never recovered from. She was the woman who refused to formally write her memoirs or a biography, and yet in the republication of her journalism selectively constructed the framework for the way Martha Gellhorn is perceived.

Using unpublished work by Gellhorn, freshly discovered archival information, interviews and letters both to and from Gellhorn, as well as my own personal interviews with Gellhorn and her contemporaries reveals a more real Martha Gellhorn. Gellhorn was a flesh and blood woman who was motivated by her own idealism, often driven to distraction by her own mythology and she is remembered as one of the brightest of her generation. In this study, Gellhorn's life and publications and her desire to control her image will further illuminate the way she is remembered. In her life she was many things: daughter, sister, mother, idealist, the Francophile, Hemingway's third wife, the novelist, the war correspondent, dowager, mythic presence, but always, Martha Gellhorn was a woman perpetually in motion.

Martha Gellhorn's World War II reportage earned her the distinction of being considered one of the finest war correspondents of the century and the conflict ultimately contributed to her best writing. Because her life was so entangled with Hemingway's, finding her way out of his shadow was neither a simple nor a clear process, and it will never be a complete process. Her life coincided with a robust period in history; she developed a voice and honed a style perfectly tailored for her subject and the times. She witnessed the times of her life and wrote about them. Her work resonates with repeated motifs: honoring the brave and true and good, and shining the light of journalism on both good and evil to bring it to the attention of the public. She was first and foremost, a writer searching in a rapidly changing world for her youthful ideals with "a cold eye and warm heart."[25]

---

[1] Caroline Moorehead, *Gellhorn: A Twentieth-Century Life* (New York: H. Holt, 2003), 424.

[2] Martha Gellhorn, *The Face of War* (New York,: Simon and Schuster, 1959), 1. Hereafter cited as *The Face of War (1959)*.

[3] Martha Gellhorn and Caroline Moorehead, *The Collected Letters of Martha Gellhorn* (New York: Henry Holt, 2007), 477; Martha Gellhorn, *Pretty Tales for Tired People* (New York: Simon and Schuster, 1965), 221.

[4] Martha Gellhorn to Angelia H. Dorman, *Unpublished Letters October 1988 - January 1998*, 21 October 1990. Hereafter cited as Gellhorn to Dorman.

[5] Gellhorn and Moorehead, *The Collected Letters of Martha Gellhorn*, 323.

[6] Jacqueline Elizabeth Orsagh to Angelia Dorman, *Discussions between Orsagh and Dorman, October 1988-April 2012*. Hereafter cited as Orsagh to Dorman.

[7] Martha Gellhorn, "Notations on *A Critical Biography of Martha Gellhorn* by Jacqueline Elizabeth Orsagh," (1989). Hereafter cited as "Martha Gellhorn notes on A Critical Biography of Martha Gellhorn by Jacqueline Elizabeth Orsagh."

[8] Bernice Kert, *The Hemingway Women* (New York: W.W. Norton, 1998).

[9] Carl E. Rollyson, *Nothing Ever Happens to the Brave: The Story of Martha Gellhorn* (New York: St. Martin's, 1990).

[10] Gellhorn to Dorman.

[11] Carl E. Rollyson, *Beautiful Exile: The Life of Martha Gellhorn* (London: Aurum Press, 2001). Carl E. Rollyson discussion with Angelia H. Dorman and Richard F. Crane at the Siena College World War II Conference, 7-9 June 1995, Albany, NY: Hereafter cited as Rollyson, Dorman, Crane.

[12] Carl E. Rollyson, *Nothing Ever Happens to the Brave: The Story of Martha Gellhorn* (New York: St. Martins, 1990), 67.

[13] Caroline Moorehead, *Gellhorn: A Twentieth-Century Life* (New York: H. Holt, 2003).

[14] Kate McLoughlin, *Martha Gellhorn: The War Writer in the Field and in the Text* (Manchester University Press, 2007).

[15] Gellhorn to Dorman (1 October 1989).

[16] Marie Colvin, *Marie Colvin on Martha Gellhorn -- The First Female War Correspondent*, BBC/Daily Motion, http://www.dailymotion.com/video/xoyt82_marie-colvin-on-martha-gellhorn-the-first-female-war-reporter_shortfilms. 2 February 2012, accessed 4 April 2012. Hereafter cited as *Marie Colvin on Martha Gellhorn*. Marie Colvin noted in her tribute to Gellhorn, just weeks before her death, that wherever she travelled she carried a copy of *The Face of War*.

[17] Martha Gellhorn, *The View from the Ground* (New York: Atlantic Monthly Press, 1988).

[18] *Marie Colvin on Martha Gellhorn.*

[19] Kate McLoughlin, *Martha Gellhorn: The War Writer in the Field and in the Text* (Manchester University Press, 2007).

[20] *Marie Colvin on Martha Gellhorn.*

[21] Roberta Ostroff, *Fire in The Wind: The Life of Dickey Chapelle* (New York: Ballantine Books, 1992).

[22] *Marie Colvin on Martha Gellhorn.*

[23] Ibid.

[24] Ibid.

[25] Kevin Kerrane and Ben Yagoda, *The Art of Fact: A Historical Anthology of Literary Journalism* (New York, NY: Scribner, 1997), 422.

CHAPTER 1

ST. LOUIS

Time and place are the cross hairs of life and have extraordinary influence on every life and Martha Gellhorn's life was no exception. Story and place and time cannot be separated. The Progressive Movement swept the United States in two waves at the end of the 19th and beginning of the 20th century. Gellhorn was born in 1908 in St. Louis at cusp of the second wave.

Progressivism was a middle class movement whose primary impetus was to reconcile the stability and values of Protestant middle class America with the tumultuous changes of the period brought on by massive immigration and in-migration to America's cities. By the turn of the 20th century, St. Louis was the fourth largest city in the nation and a city that had reinvented and almost completely rebuilt itself after the Civil War. But like other major cities St. Louis was bursting with foreign immigrants and displaced rural Americans looking for jobs and a better life, finding overcrowding, squalor and despair and the corrupt powerful machines described by Lincoln Steffans in *The Shame of the Cities*. It was this world which the work of women like Martha Gellhorn's grandmother Martha Fischel and her mother, Edna Gellhorn took place.[1]

By 1908, at the time of Martha Gellhorn's birth, Progressivism had just begun to enter its second phase, as local and national reforms were beginning to coalesce.[2] The term Progressive came into the common vocabulary in 1906, just two years before Martha

Gellhorn was born. Ironically, it was also in 1906, that Theodore Roosevelt gave his muckraker speech creating a term and a framework for the era's crusading journalists:

> There should be relentless exposure of and attack upon every evil man, whether politician or business man, every evil practice, whether in politics, business, or social life. I hail as a benefactor every writer or speaker, every man who, on the platform or in a book, magazine, or newspaper, with merciless severity makes such attack, provided always that he in his turn remembers that the attack is of use only if it is absolutely truthful.[3]

As well it provides an important way to look at Martha Gellhorn's philosophy of journalism. She wrote in 1959:

> When I was young I believed in the perfectibility of man, and in progress, and through of journalism as a guiding light. If people were told the truth, if dishonor and injustice were clearly shown to them, they would at once demand the saving action, punishment for the wrongdoers, and care for the innocent.[4]

Gellhorn does not directly mention in her public writing what action should be taken. But, she leaves no doubt that she believed that action to correct injustice would happen. Her parents and grandparents were examples of the people who fixed the problems they saw around them. This was the tableau of her early life.

The family of Edna Gellhorn's mother, Martha Ellis Fischel, came to St. Louis from Mississippi in 1860. Martha Ellis was born in 1850 and lost her mother at the age of five. She spent the first ten years of her life on the plantation with relatives before her salesman father settled in St. Louis in 1860. Much of Martha Ellis Fischel's young adulthood life was spent among the displaced Southerners relocating after the Civil War.

Martha Gellhorn's maternal grandfather, Dr. Washington (Wash) Fischel emigrated from Germany. Martha's father, George Gellhorn came to America from Austria at the turn of the century, albeit educated and a doctor, in the flood of immigration. The Fischels and Gellhorn's adjusted and accepted the norm of American life and Martha Gellhorn's grandparents worked to help immigrants assimilate, and her parents helped others do the same. They were the people who worked tirelessly to reconcile massive immigration with desired norms of middle class American life.

Progressivism was eclectic, a collection of people reacting to the problems of the day. A Progressive in Madison might be more concerned with adding the Initiative to the ballot, while a Progressive in New York City might be focused on the corruption of the political machine and yet another set of Progressives in New York City, Chicago or Philadelphia might have worked in the settlement house movement teaching English, health or citizenship classes or working as a nurses in the tenements. Some of the problems the Progressives attacked were longstanding, like the dilution of democracy and corruption of big city political machines. Others Progressives worked to counteract the problems created by massive immigration of non-Protestants from Southern and Eastern Europe and in-migration from rural areas to the cities creating burgeoning tenements. What also has to be understood is the disjointed nature of reforms in the first phase of Progressivism. It wasn't until Theodore Roosevelt's presidency that the local and national Progressive ideals coalesced and the movement was given a name. Progressivism would peak with Woodrow Wilson marking the end of the Era, a seminal time for Martha Gellhorn.

While the accomplishments of reformers like the Fischel's and the Gellhorn's were indicative of day-to-day activists and works of Progressives in cities across American, their reforms were localized. During the Progressive Era, the people with the most influence on the thinking of the nation were the writers, the muckrakers. The Progressive Era depended on media to enlighten and expose the public to what was going on in the nation, in particular in America's cities. Richard Hofstader notes that to an extraordinary degree the "Progressive mind was characteristically a journalistic mind."[5] Journalists were in a position to influence massive numbers of literate, middle class, voting Americans.

It is no surprise then that Martha Gellhorn, born at the height of the Progressive Era, would be influenced immensely by Progressive ideas of journalism. Journalists revealed the truth, called for action and were the clear catalysts for legislative and social change. Early on, Martha Gellhorn set her sights on becoming a writer like the ones admired in her home. She left St. Louis home to begin her apprenticeship in journalism in 1930 and became a full-fledged war correspondent in 1937.

Like Gellhorn, the majority of writers in the period were not particularly interested in being crusading journalists. Their goals were literary. However, the fact is that journalism was the chief occupation of the creative writers of the era. The muckrakers' realism in journalism was the flip side of literary realism. It paid for the day-to-day expenses, underwrote their literary endeavors. Likewise, Gellhorn held early parallel goals of becoming both a journalist and novelist.[6]

It was the newspapers and magazines of the Progressive Era which shined the light on the problems of the city and focused the attention of the masses. And in the end it was their commitment to realism with responsibility and the broad national audience they attracted which made magazines like *Collier's* profitable and gave them the ability to attract readers and gave journalists so much power. The rising literacy rates combined with a reduction in printing costs created a perfect storm of sorts for the crusading journalists of the time. Their articles reached substantial audiences thirsty for news and ready to crusade against social ills. This muckraking tradition of research, expose', social responsibility, and realist literature, all apply amply to Gellhorn's career.

Gellhorn's namesake and grandmother, Martha Fischel was a proto-type of the late 19th century reformer. She was a crucial part of the women's club movement, a founding member of the Missouri Federation of Women's Clubs and a leader across the spectrum of St. Louis clubs. As a co-founder of the Self- Culture Hall settlement house established in 1888, she developed a curriculum and system of training young women in domestic skills, inculcating the young women into a healthy and sanitary lifestyle and teaching them English. In 1900, her curriculum was adopted by the St. Louis Board of Education and mainstreamed into the St. Louis school system. Showing children a better way, modeling a better way, was the route to positive progressive change.[7] In those areas, Martha Fischel worked tirelessly. She believed education could change the lives of the masses. Her influence on her daughter Edna was direct. As for Martha Gellhorn, while she was not particularly close to her namesake, even though they lived in close proximity to each other, Gellhorn was still quite reverent and cognizance of the contributions of her grandmother, her place in St. Louis society and her achievements. Martha Gellhorn showed that reverence through her eulogy at Martha Fischel's funeral.

Her mother, Edna Fischel Gellhorn was Martha Gellhorn's earliest and most important role model. She was Gellhorn's closest lifelong relationship, her "moral true north" and arguably, the love of Gellhorn's life. Edna graduated from Bryn Mawr in 1900 and was elected class president for life. In her travels she raised over $1 million for Bryn Mawr and served on the advisory board for the college.[8] She married George Gellhorn in 1903, and their first son George Jr. was born in 1904, Walter in 1905, Martha in 1908 and Alfred in 1912.[9]

By all accounts, Edna Gellhorn was a tireless reformer. She worked for whatever it was she saw as needing reform. Early on in her young adulthood, her efforts were varied, from smoke abatement, safe milk for children and as noted "finally found her cause with women's voting rights."[10] In 1907, she began the work that would define her public service career in St. Louis with the St. Louis Equal Suffrage League. She in time became president of the organization and eventually took on a national leadership role in the League of Women's voters.

Education in and use of the process of democracy became the axis for much of Edna's energy, with suffrage being the primary focus. Martha Gellhorn's early life was full of the example of her parents and grandparents activism. Also their model was one of constantly attempting to teach others by showing them a better way of life. This is a recurrent theme in Gellhorn's writing and in her discourses with others.[11]

Edna believed whole-heartedly that the vote for women could make a real difference in accomplishing change. Suffrage in St. Louis was a very conservative endeavor, yet the participants as mild mannered as they were, were considered radical. Edna was described by Emily Newell Blair as the "Brunhild of the suffragists." [12] In St. Louis the thin line between the expectations of middle class women and pushing that boundary for the vote is indicative of the movement nationwide. While it is sometimes overlooked Edna was integrally involved in the "Walkless-Talkless Parade" or the better known "The Golden Lane" protest. The Golden Lane Protest is perhaps one of the most well known non-violent political demonstrations for the vote outside of Washington DC. The Golden Lane Protest was a deliberate attempt to conservatively get the most attention possible for the cause of women's suffrage. Coinciding with the 1916 Democratic National Convention in St. Louis the plan was to line the streets with women in white, with yellow sashes and parasols. With the major attention of the convention on the whether or not to pass a ban on alcohol and the debate regarding the war in Europe, the goal was to garner enough attention to get a women's suffrage plank in the platform. This was a precarious goal. Without the vote, what power did women have to force the issue to the forefront?[13] However, the power of 7,000 women in white could not be denied. In the end there was a bitter fight, Edna noted:

> We decided we didn't want to have a parade but we did want to be noticed…so thousands of us in yellow sashes and carrying yellow parasols lined both sides of Locust Street…[14]

But it was the tableau which Edna recalled as being most memorable; women representing states were draped with various colored sashes, white for those with the vote, gray for partial suffrage and black for those without any type of suffrage for women.[15] Prominent were two girls, symbolizing the future, one of whom was the organizer Edna's daughter, young Martha. Through out Gellhorn's life Edna was always Martha's touchstone and her primary role model.

For most of the first 12 years of Martha's life, Edna was vigorously involved in the crusade for suffrage. This was followed by lengthy tours throughout the country to raise voter awareness and membership in the League of Women Voters. Later in her life, Edna credited her housekeeping staff for allowing her the freedom to devote herself to her various civic endeavors.[16] Throughout her life, Martha never complained or seemed to notice that her mother and father were often absent in the pursuit of their passions. This speaks to Edna's ability to manage her housekeeping staff, keep a schedule and pattern of normalcy, in spite of the frequent absences of herself and her husband, George Gellhorn. Gellhorn seems to have attempted to emulate this in her later non-traditional role as a mother. It is clear that the Gellhorns made a point to compensate for lost time with as much family-dinner time as possible and with excursions on the weekends. Martha recalled the dinner table as being crucial in her development. From her interviews with Gellhorn, Orsagh wrote about the Gellhorn household in her dissertation, noting that there were "rules" in the Gellhorn household:

> Rule Number One: People are people. None of their guests were to be designated by religion, race or sex. One was not permitted to say "that Negro woman," "Jewish man," or "Spanish person." No labels. … Money…was not to be discussed. Rule Number Two outlawed it as a value in the Gellhorn household.[17]

Keeping to "Rule Number One" was not always easy for Martha Gellhorn. While it is probable that she believed she was color blind, her observation of race, class and color were often very unflattering to those she wrote about and by extension to herself. While on one hand she felt she was enlightened and forward thinking about race, class and gender, Martha Gellhorn's words at times begged to differ. This is especially so when Martha Gellhorn was writing about

China, the Caribbean, the Southern United States and Africa. "Rule Number Two" was easier for Gellhorn to keep, but it is always far easier for those with the money to dismiss its value.

Edna's involvement in the cause of suffrage on both the local and national level cannot be discounted. Later, the FBI described her as "active in agitation for women suffrage… and regarded as slightly radical," but her ability to walk the thin line between action and radicalism is attested to by the esteem in which she was held by the various suffrage organizations and her future as a guiding force in the League of Women's Voters. In fact, there was a disconnection between the conservative suffragists and the more radical suffragists.[18]

In a 1964 speech, Edna looked back on the importance of Anna Howard Shaw and in an attempt to educate the younger generation of women, she mentions Alice Paul's involvement in passing and lightly jokes that they were let out of jail because they were too much trouble. Edna contrasted "trouble" versus "the reality" which was the Occoquan workhouse experience for those suffragists involved with the National Women's Party. Edna's view of the struggle for suffrage was what she saw only in her personal experience. Edna did not appreciate the violence of their arrests, the hunger strikes and violent force feeding.[19] The violent head busting protest did not register on Edna's middle-class sensibilities; neither would they have registered as such on Martha. Martha's view of the struggle for suffrage was haloed by the conservative, logical, "decent" path followed by the majority of suffragists like her mother and her later close friend Eleanor Roosevelt. Edna and Mrs. Roosevelt's examples were that if one acted appropriately, brought problems out into the light, people would see the problems and correct them.

Martha Gellhorn restates her belief firmly, noting "If people were told the truth, if dishonor and injustice were clearly shown to them, they would at once demand the saving action, punishment of wrong-doers, and care for the innocent"[20] Gellhorn's early and personal experiences were not those of seeing her mother put in jail and abused. Martha observed Edna's logical decent manner and her hard work achieved her ends, the vote. Martha's view was obscured by her mother's conservative example and she did not fully appreciate the potential violence which it often took to accomplish social change. It was a deceptively simplistic idea and led Martha Gellhorn to be a deceptively simplistic instructor in both her writing and to younger people, doling out sage often simple advice.[21]

Martha Gellhorn's relationship with her father was more complex. Whereas Martha and Edna had a deep and unspoken bond, Dr. Gellhorn was a loving but cooler character. Receiving his medical training in Breslau, George Gellhorn arrived in St. Louis with a letter of introduction to Dr. Washington "Wash" Fischel. Fischel was a distinguished physician and professor of clinical medicine at Washington University. In addition, he was a founder of the Barnard Free Skin and Cancer Hospital. George worked closely with his father-in-law Dr. Washington "Wash" Fischel. They both believed in and stressed health, family togetherness and activity, and intellectual curiosity. He had in common with George Gellhorn foreign roots; Fischel's family was from Prague.

Martha was very captivated by the story of her father's arrival in the Fischel house, delivering the letter of introduction and then seeing Edna float down the staircase like an angel. As Jacqueline Orsagh wrote describing George Gellhorn's journey to America, it was one that ended in a "the straight line destination of a nineteenth century novel."[22] Three years after her graduation from Bryn Mawr, Edna and George were married.

Martha's memory of her parents and their relationship was enamored with a soft romantic flair. She remembered them as a loving, devoted couple. Her father's view of Edna was always romantic and she obviously brought out the best in him, the softer side. Her parents' marriage was idealized. She saw it as built on mutual respect and admiration. Not unlike Martha's lack of notice of her parents' absences, it is likely she was not exposed to the give and take of their relationship. They were the portrait of the ideal. Marriage was something Gellhorn never understood. She was unable to share that type of complex long lasting intimate interpersonal relationship with a man.[23]

Gellhorn's parents were not satisfied with the educational options available for their children and they became part of a core group of upper middle class Progressive parents responsible for the founding of the John Burroughs School in St. Louis. One of the Gellhorn's core ideas was that all schools should be experimental and allow students to explore learning through drama, poetry, the arts, as well as mathematics and science. Under the leadership of William M. Aikin, the John Burroughs School developed into a working model of Progressive educational ideology. Aikin remained at Burroughs throughout the time the Gellhorn children attended the school, moving on in 1935 to chair the Eight Year Study Project. During the Gellhorn children's time at the John Burroughs School, the curriculum was rigorous and experiential. The curriculum was focused on the relevance of the material in relationship to the student, making it a student-centered learning environment.[24] Martha was an active student in drama and writing contributing poems and stories to the literary magazine of the school.

Martha completed her secondary education at John Burroughs School and then followed in her mother's footsteps and went east to Bryn Mawr. By all accounts Gellhorn was a good student, yet she failed her first set of Bryn Mawr entrance exams. Whether she was not ready to leave St. Louis or possibly hesitated to follow so many of her other St. Louis friends to Bryn Mawr is impossible to know.

Bryn Mawr was an imperfect fit from the start. Gellhorn was not particularly interested in finishing her studies at Bryn Mawr, in spite of or because of the fact that her mother was a distinguished graduate and active alumnus. The sense is that as much as she loved and respected her mother, she went along with Bryn Mawr for as long as it took her to fully plan an escape. Martha was not Edna and her level of impatience is clearly visible in her choice to quit college one year short of completion. Carl Rollyson describes Gellhorn during this period as rebellious as evidenced by her smoking and being perceived as "sophisticated" by her peers. Her time at Bryn Mawr was marked by modest rebellion and challenges to the required regimentation of the student body. He goes on to say that the last thing Gellhorn wanted was to "'come out' to society."[25]

There is little doubt that Martha Gellhorn's early life was full of romantic fancies. As much as she became the battle-toughened war correspondent, underlying that was the idealism of a romantic and the distance of the privileged. As a teen, she saw herself as a poet at John Burroughs and studied French at Bryn Mawr. She was engrossed in the work of the "lost generation" and clearly begins to imagine herself in her own romantic version of Hemingway's expatriate Paris, supporting herself as a journalist and living the life of the artist in Paris. In short time, she made it to Paris and immersed herself in all life and things French.

The decision to leave Bryn Mawr meant finding a job and a way to support her decision. To prepare for the transition from student to self-supporting young woman, Gellhorn began writing newspapers in search of a job. It was not her nature, nor the way she was raised to make a decision and expect her parents to pay for that luxury. Her father was especially disappointed that she was quitting school and was not keen to support her decision financially. It is uncertain how many newspapers and magazines Gellhorn applied to. The pedigree of an upper middle class Bryn Mawr girl was not exactly what most small daily papers were looking for. They wanted and needed reporters, not debutantes. As the Emporia Gazette wrote to Gellhorn, they needed "writers who could spell local names" and knew the differences between cattle breeds.[26]

She did line up work. Her first job after dropping out of college was in the summer with the *New Republic* as a manuscript reader. She was in New York City, staying with friends, surrounded by luminaries of the day like Edmund Wilson and Walter Lippman. But she was the bottom of the heap, a coffee girl, and she describes her time there as feeling like an "extension of Bryn Mawr," probably because she leaned so hard on her connections from Bryn Mawr and St. Louis to get the job.[27] And while the Midwestern newspapers rejected her because of her upper middle class background, the job her background provided her at the *New Republic* with was the last thing she wanted. Regardless of hobnobbing with literary luminaries at the *New Republic* and the opportunity to publish a trite article on Rudee Vallee, Gellhorn moved on as soon as she could secure a job elsewhere. In addition to being a venue for publishing two very early articles, *The New Republic* provided Gellhorn a venue to publish half a dozen more articles in the mid-1950s.[28]

While Gellhorn's dream was to be in Paris, her journey to Paris was made via a detour to Albany, NY. In Albany in November,

1929, she was hired as a girl cub reporter on *The Albany Times Union*, a Hearst paper for which she covered "the morgue and the ladies clubs." Gellhorn found her initiation in the mostly male world of newspaper journalism quite intoxicating in more than one sense, recalling:

> The managing editor was drunk; the whole staff was drunk. We were fired regularly once a day and we'd go into a speakeasy and wait until they'd call us back. Word crept out that perhaps this was not the best ambience for a well-brought-up girl from Bryn Mawr.[29]

Gellhorn loved the job at the Times Union. In 1980, she nostalgically recalled "I never enjoyed anything more in my life!" Gellhorn also notably later said that "the world she loved was one of 'men, and not men and women'" and in Albany she was immersed in the world of men, newspapermen, no less.[30] It was also an immersion into the real and gritty world outside of familiar St. Louis. It was an opportunity to experience life on that level and in her mind to provide grist for the mill that was to launch her literary career.

But, it was due to this "Front Page" scenario that Gellhorn's mother arranged for Martha's first meeting with Eleanor Roosevelt. Edna Gellhorn, still reeling from her daughter's decision to quit Bryn Mawr in her junior year, contacted her friend from the League of Women's Voters and First Lady of New York to check up on young Martha. The object of this motherly solicitude reacted with predictable resentment: "I was probably sullen about the whole thing, departed, quickly, and forgot all about it."[31] Obviously, all girl reporters covering the morgues were not invited to the Governor's mansion. However, this is just one of many instances of the

Gellhorn's family standing resulting in patronage for their daughter. Gellhorn worked for *The Albany Times Union* for six months before she reluctantly returned to St. Louis, primarily because of her family's concerns about her working situation in Albany.

St. Louis was not where she wanted to be. It was an exercise in misery for Gellhorn and a test of patience for her parents. Gellhorn secretly rented a room and spent her time writing. It was also a period of time for Gellhorn to renew and cultivate acquaintances with the staff of *The St. Louis Post Dispatch*. During her youth, St. Louis was a place she always needed to escape. Later in Martha's life, St. Louis was an inconvenience she endured in order to spend time with her beloved mother.[32]

If Edna was concerned about her daughter in Albany frequenting the morgues and carousing with hard drinking reporters, Martha's departure for Paris was cause for even greater concern. By her account she secured her passage on the Holland Line in exchange for "glowing article" to use in their trade magazine.[33] Her mother gave her $75, enough to last her about 3 months if managed wisely. She attempted to find work by walking into the Paris bureau of the *New York Times* in early 1931 and as she recalled announced herself to the bureau chief "that she was prepared to start work as a foreign correspondent on his staff."[34] That brash entry did not secure her a post on *The New York Times*. She was not the first girl from Bryn Mawr, or for that matter St. Louis, who had arrived in Paris with lofty ideas of becoming a writer. But her confidence combined with personable manners, charm and youthful enthusiasm helped Gellhorn make friends in Paris and enough professional contacts to make a start toward her goal and garnered her a few free lunches along the way.[35]

The considerable travel during the early 1930s provided the observant young Martha with an extensive exposure to the complexities of the people and political situations of the time in Europe.[36] What she lacked in disciplined study, she made up for with this immersion into the world of the French and her travels in Europe. Her free-lance work from this period is predominately found in *The St. Louis Post Dispatch*, and ranges from fashion stories to articles on the women at the League of Nations.[37]

During this free-lance period, she made just enough money writing to support herself and her travels. It is important to remember that Gellhorn always had the security of her parents. Gellhorn seldom mentions the fact that her parents were always there to bail her out of an untenable situation. This is probably because she chose not to rely on them, at the same time it is important to recognize that that safety net and affluence allowed for bold moves on her part.

---

[1] Jim Willis, *100 Media Moments That Changed America* (Santa Barbara, Calif.: Greenwood Press, 2010), 46.

[2] Robert H. Wiebe, *The Search for Order, 1877-1920* (Westport, Conn.: Greenwood Press, 1980), 198.

[3] Theodore Roosevelt, "The Man with the Muck-Rake (1906)," in *American Rhetoric* (http://www.americanrhetoric.com/speeches/teddyrooseveltmuckrake.htm n.d.Web, accessed 1 September 2011.

[4] Martha Gellhorn, *The Face of War* (New York: Atlantic Monthly Press, 1988), 1. Hereafter cited as *The Face of War* (1988).

[5] Richard Hofstadter, *The Age of Reform: From Bryan to F. D. R.* (New York: Knopf, 1955), 186.

[6] Ibid., 198-99.

[7] Katharine T. Corbett, *In Her Place: A Guide to St. Louis Women's History* (St. Louis: Missouri Historical Society Press, 1999), 233.

[8] "Bryn Mawr Women as Suffragists: The NAWSA Alumnae," Bryn Mawr Library Special Collections, http://www.brynmawr.edu/library/exhibits/suffrage/nawsaAlums.html#tableau. n.d. accessed 14 April 2012.

[9] Moorehead, *Gellhorn: A Twentieth-Century Life*, 14.

[10] *Experiencing Women's History in Missouri: Edna Gellhorn.* n.d. Web accessed 12 April 2012.

[11] Martha Gellhorn, Interviewed by Angelia Dorman, London, 14 June 1995. Hereafter cited as Gellhorn Interview.

[12] Karen Graves, *Girls' Schooling During the Progressive Era: From Female Scholar to Domesticated Citizen*, Garland Reference Library of Social Science (New York: Garland Pub., 1998), 77-81; Emily Newell Blair, Virginia Jeans Laas, and ebrary Inc., *Bridging Two Eras: The Autobiography of Emily Newell Blair, 1877-1951* (Columbia: University of Missouri Press, 1999), 205.

[13] Sean McLachlan, *It Happened in Missouri* (Guilford, Conn: Globe Pequot Press, 2008), 93-95.

[14] "Bryn Mawr Women as Suffragists: The NAWSA Alumnae."

[15] Ibid.

[16] *Experiencing Women's History in Missouri: Edna Gellhorn.*

[17] Jacqueline Elizabeth Orsagh, *A Critical Biography of Martha Gellhorn* (Michigan State University, 1978), 7. Also, Martha Gellhorn, "Notations on *A Critical Biography of Martha Gellhorn* by Jacqueline Elizabeth Orsagh," (1989). Orsagh undertook the first critical study of Martha Gellhorn's life and work. Orsagh and Gellhorn corresponded and eventually Gellhorn agreed to meet with her over a period of several days for interviews. In December 1989, I sent Gellhorn a copy of the dissertation. She made comments and revisions and the commentary and revisions were mailed by Gellhorn to me. Gellhorn's notations on

Orsagh's dissertation are Hereafter cited as "Gellhorn notations on *A Critical Biography of Martha Gellhorn.*"

[18] Don Edward Harley, "Walter Gellhorn FBI File SL File No. 101-603-2-43."

[19] *Experiencing Women's History in Missouri: Edna Gellhorn.*

[20] Gellhorn, *The Face of War (1988),* 1.

[21] Gellhorn Interview, 21 June 1995.

[22] Orsagh, *A Critical Biography of Martha Gellhorn,* 2.

[23] Gellhorn was close to a number of friends who were involved in long term relationships, like that of her former teacher Hortense Flexner, and her friends Diana Cooper and Virginia Cowles.

[24] J.W. Wrightstone, *Appraisal of Experimental High School Practices* (Teachers College, Columbia University, 1936), 33.

[25] Rollyson, *Nothing Ever Happens to the Brave: The Story of Martha Gellhorn,* 26.

[26] Emily Williams, "Oral History Interview: Martha Gellhorn," (St. Moritz Hotel: Franklin Delano Roosevelt Library, 20 February 1980), 66 pages. Hereafter cited as FDR Oral History Project.

[27] Ibid.

[28] Gellhorn, Notations on *A Critical Biography of Martha Gellhorn,* 12.

[29] FDR Oral History Project.

[30] Martha Gellhorn and Caroline Moorehead, *The Collected Letters of Martha Gellhorn* (New York: Henry Holt, 2006), 717.

[31] FDR Oral History Project.

[32] After Edna Gellhorn's death, Martha had no reason to ever return to St. Louis.

[33] Martha Gellhorn, *The View from the Ground* (New York: Atlantic Monthly Press, 1988), 66.

[34] Ibid and Martha Gellhorn Interview, 11 August 1991.

[35] Gellhorn, *The View from the Ground*, 66.

[36] Ibid., 67.

[37] Gellhorn's articles showed up regularly in a number of small French publications, and occasionally in an American magazine or on the wire service. The majority of her work from this period can be found in *The St. Louis Post-Dispatch. The Post-Dispatch* provided her with a regular outlet for her freelance articles.

CHAPTER 2

GELLHORN'S EUROPE IN THE 1930S

"When you were very young what interested you was France, and you found or were found by the most complete Frenchman available. Then you were interested in writing, so you found or were found by what you thought the finest writer. In the war, you were interested in bravery and you found or were found by who was considered perhaps the bravest of all." [1]

—Edna Gellhorn to Martha Gellhorn

Like most of her generation, Gellhorn had read Hemingway and if she had been in search of Jake Barnes's Paris, she was not to find it. Paris was no longer the Paris of the Lost Generation. While Gertrude Stein and Sylvia Beach were still in Paris, the avant-garde had changed. It was no longer the romantic rose colored 1920s Paris of Hemingway's *A Movable Feast*. It was more Henry Miller's Paris, grittier, less romantic, more real and surreal. Lee Miller arrived in this Paris in 1929 and began the work with Man Ray which resulted in their development of solarization and her early portfolio of surrealist photography. [2] It was this Paris that Gellhorn found on her arrival. It is also this Paris in which she lives. [3]

Almost immediately after her recollection of her comic entrée to Paris, in *The View from the Ground*, Gellhorn notes:

Unlike the gifted Americans and British who settled in Paris in the twenties and lived among each other in what seems to me a cozy literary world, I soon lived entirely among the

35

French, not a cozy world. The men were politicians and political journalists, the students of my generation were just as fervently political.[4]

It was a heady time for young Marty Gellhorn from St. Louis. During this period, she became associated with a young upper class Frenchman, Bertrand de Jouvenel. De Jouvenel was a young political Frenchman who happened to be the famed author Colette's stepson and erstwhile lover. De Jouvenel was a seminal force in Gellhorn's life during this period. Bertrand was the son of Henry de Jouvenel an upper class writer, journalist, diplomat and gentleman and his mother was journalist Claire Boas.

Gellhorn's relationship with Bertrand de Jouvenel was topsy turvy. Prior to the publication of Carl Rollyson's *Nothing Ever Happens to the Brave,* very few people outside of the scholarly world were familiar with de Jouvenel and Martha took great exception to the fact that Rollyson contended they were married. It was an honest mistake on the part of Rollyson. The relationship was complex; it was very French. De Jouvenel was married to another woman who had no intention of granting him a divorce, and de Jouvenel chased madly after Gellhorn on two continents.

While much is made of de Jouvenel's relationship with his step-mother Collette, his contributions to political thought are far more interesting and important. Of all of Gellhorn's liaisons, de Jouvenel was the great thinker and he, too, is in the thick of his times. Gellhorn wrote much of her first novel at de Jouvenel's house in La Favière and through de Jouvenel she met influential politicians, artists and writers. Off and on for four years Gellhorn maintained a relationship with de Jouvenel much to the chagrin of her father.

Also, during this period Gellhorn, along with de Jouvenel, became involved in the European pacifist movement. This period served as a journalistic apprenticeship for Gellhorn and de Jouvenel was her companion and a critical part of her education in the politics of Europe in the early 1930s.[5] Along with his set of acquaintances, Gellhorn became relatively well known amongst the non-Marxist left.

During the midst of their affair in 1931, the couple presented themselves in St. Louis. It was the *St. Louis Post- Dispatch* which published that they were "married."[6] Later in her life, Gellhorn did nothing to really clarify their marital or relationship status. As much as she was incensed about it, she was equally indignant about making any clarification of the situation.[7] The two travelled across the U.S. in the fall with Gellhorn introducing de Jouvenel to America. It was a pleasure trip as the two motored through the US. It is also on this trip which the seeds of controversial *Justice at Night* were sown.

Justice at Night is one of Gellhorn's most controversial pieces of writing. The article appeared in the *New Republic* as non-fiction. In *The View From the Ground*, Gellhorn's commentary on the article was:

> I remembered "Justice at Night" suddenly; it emerged intact, from its burial in my brain, and wrote itself as if by Ouija board on sunny morning in London in the summer of 1936. I don't know if it belongs here since it is not direct reporting; recollection in tranquility four and a half years late…That morning to show him (H.G. Wells) that I could write if I felt like it, I sat in his garden and let "Justice at Night" produce itself. Wells sent it on to the Spectator. I had already moved on to Germany where I ceased being a pacifist and became an ardent anti-Fascist.[8]

However, the article is a composite of incidents Gellhorn heard about, not that she witnessed. There are two versions of the story of the publication of *Justice at Night*; both illuminate seldom discussed aspects of Gellhorn. One version is the one above; the other is recounted in Moorehead from one of Gellhorn's letters. Gellhorn's insists:

> Around now, I feel that I have attended twenty lynchings and I wish I'd never seen fit to while away a morning doing a piece of accurate guessing." In this account, she said that she had fused two separate incidents—meeting a drunken truck driver on his way home from a lynching, and, later, talking to a man whose son had been lynched—into a single story. Mrs. Roosevelt advised her to say nothing and let it all blow over.[9]

She allowed it to blow over, but made a deliberate decision in 1988 to include the article in *The View From the Ground*. Gellhorn was not only capable of youthful journalistic deception, she was also capable of deliberately continuing that deception and adding it to her self selected canon of work. Something deep within Gellhorn's ego obviously called out to her to republish the article. In the end she could not let go of the article and refused to actually clarify the circumstances surrounding the article. She allowed the deception for whatever reasons. While it does not call the veracity of all of her work in to question, it does add to the case that Gellhorn had a need to control her image at a high personal cost. She cannot have believed this fictitious article would not be exposed. Perhaps, she believed her explanation in *The View From the Ground* would be enough to exonerate the error.

The article itself reads more like an omitted chapter from Gellhorn's Depression novel, *The Trouble I've Seen*. Gellhorn is over the top with her lynching story. Not only does she assert that a Southern lynch mob leader would be pleasantly concerned with their situation, willing to share his liquor and bring two outsiders along to watch the mob not only lynch "Hyacinth," but to immolate him after his neck is broken. Concluding the piece, Gellhorn writes:

> The driver and the man with the bottle came back to the truck and got in. They seemed in a good frame of mind. The driver said, "Well there won't be no more fresh niggers in these parts for a while. We'll get you to Columbia now. Sorry we had ta (sic) keep you waiting…"[10]

The great lengths Gellhorn went to in order to keep the article classified as a piece of her journalism, indicate an inability to reconcile her errors in judgment in spite of her commitment to truthfulness in journalism. It echoes her later desire to correct biography, but not clarify the needed correction. As with Carl Rollyson's assertion of her marriage to de Jouvenel, she pathologically refused to explain any thing regarding the error. While she knew there were notices of their being married in the *St. Louis Post Dispatch* and she was called the Marquise de Jouvenel in print, she would not comment on their relationship. Nor did she feel the need to explain the fact that they had deliberately misled the press in order for Gellhorn's relationship with de Jouvenel to be acceptable to St. Louis society and avoid embarrassing her parents with her lifestyle choices. At the same time, she vilified Rollyson for his honest mistake. This irrational double standard also becomes a factor later when she discusses her life with Hemingway.

To say that Dr. Gellhorn was not fond of de Jouvenel is an understatement. Her affair with de Jouvenel caused an estrangement between the two and added a great deal of stress to Dr. Gellhorn and Edna's relationship. Dr. Gellhorn describes the relationship between Martha and de Jouvenel "as your affair with that little French runt that gave you so much valuable experience and us so much real pain."[11] Dr. Gellhorn was not pleased with Martha's flitting about and felt she needed to take her life and herself more seriously.

Despite Dr. Gellhorn's assessment of de Jouvenel, he was quite a figure in his own right. After serving for a brief period as Czechoslovakian President Eduard Benes personal secretary, he stood for Parliament at age 23 as a Radical-Socialist. He drifted into pacifism and then into a right wing populism. His split with French Right Wing politics came with their support for the Munich Pact. In response, he joined French Army intelligence, in opposition to the impending Nazis. After the French armistice with Germany, he worked for the resistance, eventually fleeing to Switzerland to avoid the Gestapo. After the war he concentrated on his political writing.[12] De Jouvenel's theories on power and economics felt that politics "must actively promote civic friendship, but at the same time…resist all forms of primitivist and communitarian nostalgia." His goals are lofty and broad. In his writing, he attempts to come to an understanding of the basic fundamental nature of politics, its development along with the character of leadership, and by analyzing its roots, attempts to formulate a path for a political future.[13]

While travelling with Gellhorn across the U.S. in 1931 and later in August of 1935, De Jouvenel researched and formulated his theories about America. Lesser known, he is often compared to de Tocqueville, but this is problematic to the modern reader who only knows de Tocqueville from their high school history classes and his descriptions of American democracy. De Jouvenel's theories had the advantage of a 20th century perspective. From which, de Jouvenel is able to broaden the base of his theories in light of the practical analysis of communism, fascism, and democracies. He uses both intellectual history and the modern world to formulate a more contemporary view of modern societies, their nature, their structures of power and their effectiveness. There is no doubt that de Jouvenel learned a great deal about America from Gellhorn and in turn he added greatly to Gellhorn's political education.

In the spring of 1934, Gellhorn had a first hand look at Nazi German brutality and realized that she and Bertrand held differing views on the issue of appeasing the Nazis. In 1934, she was the only woman with a group of pacifists, mainly from the Sorbonne, who traveled to Berlin to meet with the young National Socialists and Hitler Youth leader Baldur von Schirach. Gellhorn says of the Nazis, "they proved to have one parrot brain among the lot and we did not care for them."[14] Motivated by the guilt many liberals felt about the postwar treatment of Germany and their pacifist beliefs, the group tried to excuse the attitudes of the young Nazis. She adds, writing in 1959, "I was a pacifist and it interfered with my principles to use my eyes."[15] It was not the only time that Gellhorn would suffer from principled blindness. Later in her life, there are instances where she clung so tightly to political ideals that they interfered with her ability to assess and absorb complexity of Cold War situations.

Gellhorn booked passage to the United States in the fall of 1934. She said that she felt it was time to come home and do something to help her own country, but it is hard to determine whether that was as much the case as it was the time for Gellhorn to change scenery in her life and leave de Jouvenel behind. She remained fond of de Jouvenel. She mentions him more than a year later in a long letter to Pauline Hemingway in which included a photo and more detailed physical description of "Bertrand."[16] With the exception of his long visit tin the summer of 1935, de Jouvenel and Gellhorn were out of touch until after World War II. At that point, she rekindled her friendship with him. By that time de Jouvenel was remarried and absorbed in his scholarly endeavors. They maintained their friendship until his death in 1987.

Gellhorn's most memorable article from this period is a profile for the *St. Louis Post Dispatch* on the women of the League of Nations, *Geneva Portrait: Glimpses of the Women Delegates to the League of Nations.* It is a woman's angle article primarily a profile of one woman, Mademoiselle (Mlle.) Forchhammer of Denmark. The article touches on some of Mlle. Forchhammer's activities dealing with humanitarian issues, and serious women's issues, namely "the protection of women and children in the Near East" and also "the white slave traffic."[17] In many ways, Gellhorn's profile reflects a reformer the same age and with a character much like her grandmother. Possibly the part of the article with most importance in discussing Gellhorn is the commentary reflecting her feelings on feminism:

> It would not occur to Mlle Forchhammer to make an issue of herself as a woman; she is a human being living in the twentieth century with certain obligations and certain abilities. There were (and perhaps still are) two school of feminist; one of which said, "Let's deny our femininity!" The other of which said, "Let us trade on it." And then there are people like Mlle Forchhammer who ignore the whole question. They are the effective ones. [18]

It is a very idealistic immature notion of feminism, which changes little during Gellhorn's life. It is as if ignoring being a woman changes the fact that being a woman has an effect. It is similar to Gellhorn's rejection of her St. Louis social status and her inability to recognizing the fact that she had an outlet to publish her articles and make money directly due to her social standing in St. Louis. Just below the title and byline, but above the text of the article is the note that "This is the second of a series of articles by

Miss Gellhorn, who is the daughter of Dr. and Mrs. George Gellhorn of St. Louis." [19]

In addition to her journalism, Martha completed her first, very weak, novel in late 1933. This was the beginning her life-long pattern of a dual fiction/non-fiction career, in which she used her journalism to support herself while writing fiction, and as a well to draw upon for use in her fiction. Although it is an immature literary work, *What Mad Pursuit* is one of the few female initiation stories in American literature.[20] Jacqueline Orsagh noted that it also demonstrates a thematic pattern which reappears throughout her later work: "the problem of living a vital life when surrounded by a mechanical existence, the need for independent women to find both fulfillment and companionship, and the quest for justice in a world of compromise and inequality."[21]

What Mad Pursuit is a glimpse into young Martha Gellhorn's mind, her thoughts and fantasies. It is her first foray into fiction and she melds the experiences of Martha Gellhorn with her main character, Charis Day. Charis is a character based entirely on Gellhorn and the story is fantasy she created about a young crusader out to see the world and save it. Charis is larger than the personality of Martha Gellhorn and Gellhorn's use of Charis's character informs a great deal of what Gellhorn thought about herself one push beyond whom she really was. This is also an early instance of Gellhorn beginning to shape the mythology of her own character. Whether Gellhorn quit Bryn Mawr over her claimed "boredom" or to break away from a life more like her Mother's or to escape a perceived path of life she would not be able to control if she had continued Bryn Mawr is unknown. But, Gellhorn did not quit in idealistic protest over an unfair expulsion like Charis.

Like Martha Gellhorn, Charis is unable to find real love along the way. However, the book does attempt moments of gritty realism, but even those are sometimes a stretch. Charis is hiking the Pyrenees and breaks out in a rash on her chest, like Martha Gellhorn did at one time. Martha Gellhorn believed that she had syphilis, but it was only prickly heat. Gellhorn saddled Charis with syphilis in the story. It is an attempt at gritty realism, but the tone and the story are strained and somewhat comical. The entire book misses the mark. As Gellhorn said in later years to young authors "it can be a blessing not having your first (bad) novel published. I wish mine hadn't been."[22] Gellhorn also deleted it from her list of published works.

Dr. Gellhorn was unimpressed by *What Mad Pursuit*. He was disturbed by Gellhorn's life since she left St. Louis and had concerns regarding Martha's future. Carolyn Moorehead quotes one of the few existing letters from Dr. Gellhorn to Martha:

> It will be pretty dark for you if you remain in the groove you have been ploughing these past six or seven years. Strangely, that has been the only thing you haven't got tired of, this self-deceptions...I am ready to bet that many of the people who are now fascinated by you would be rather surprised, I mean disillusioned, if they knew that you are almost 27 years old. The impression of a precocious and altogether bewitching child would vanish...It's you and only you that can pull you out of this slough of self-pity and self-abasement and make you a person of lasting worth...'I want to write, I want to write' that is your eternal wail. Then why the devil don't you? If you really want to write, write by all means, but do it NOW...instead of capitalizing on your yellow hair and your lively, spicy conversation, you should have the pride of wanting to show the world that you can hold your place with anybody else, not only while you are young and attractive to men, but at any time.[23]

It is clear that Martha Gellhorn had an idea of who and what she wanted to be, but she struggled with her own ability to be sidetracked and to trade on her looks and charm. Ironically, many of Dr. Gellhorn's issues and concerns will be brought up again to Martha by Ernest Hemingway in 1943.

---

[1] Moorehead, *Gellhorn : A Twentieth-Century Life*, 231.

[2] Carolyn Burke, *Lee Miller: A Life* (Knopf, 2005), 74. Lee Miller was a year and a half older than Gellhorn and began her career in New York as a fashion model for Conde Nast. Miller left New York for Paris to pursue an artistic life. She became a part of the Surrealist movement, and later became a very in demand portrait photographer and fashion photographer. When World War II began, she persuaded *Vogue* to allow her to cover the war. Miller provided articles and photographic images which rivaled and surpassed another Gellhorn contemporary Margaret Bourke-White of *Life Magazine*.

[3] For a more detailed account of Paris during this period see William Wiser, *The Twilight Years: Paris in the 1930s* (Robson Books, 2001). Gellhorn romanticizes her arrival in France in The View from the Ground. The beginning of her version of her arrival in Paris reads like a brisk scene from a Katherine Hepburn comedy of the early 1930s. By her account, after settling in she waltzed in to the editor of *The New York Times* and asked for a job as a foreign correspondent. She was laughed at by the editor probably as much for the naïve presumptuousness as the fact she was living in a maison de passé and was not aware of it.

[4] Gellhorn, *The View from the Ground*, 67.

[5] Gellhorn, *The Face of War (1959)*, 9-10.

[6] Rollyson, *Nothing Ever Happens to the Brave*, 67.

[7] Gellhorn, Interview, 21 June 1995.

[8] Gellhorn, *The View from the Ground*, 68-69.

[9] Moorehead, *Gellhorn: A Twentieth-Century Life*, 95.

[10] Gellhorn, *The View from the Ground*, 9.

[11] Moorehead, *Gellhorn: A Twentieth-Century Life*, 89.

[12] Brian C. Anderson, "Bertrand de Jouvenel's Melancholy Liberalism," *Public Interest*, No. 143 (2001): 90.

[13] Noël O'Sullivan, *Political Theory in Transition* (New York: Routledge, 2000), 133

[14] *The Face of War (1959)*, 14.

[15] Ibid.

[16] Gellhorn and Moorehead, *The Collected Letters of Martha Gellhorn*, 54.

[17] Martha Gellhorn, "Geneva Portraits," *St. Louis Post Dispatch* 20 November 1930, 2D.

[18] Ibid.

[19] Ibid.

[20] Orsagh, *A Critical Biography of Martha Gellhorn*, 19.

[21] Ibid., 22.

[22] Gellhorn Interview, 28 February 1990.

[23] Moorehead, *Gellhorn: A Twentieth-Century Life*, 89.

CHAPTER 3

WORKING FOR THE NEW DEAL

While Gellhorn was in Europe, Franklin Roosevelt ran for president in 1932 on vague promises to bring relief to Americans suffering from the greatest economic crisis in American History. Roosevelt put together an ad hoc eclectic group of individuals from all walks of life and areas of experience to confront the crisis at hand. These were not Progressives per se, nor were they as often envisioned as a bureaucratic elite. They had however all come of age in the Progressive era and were very much people of their time. They ranged the spectrum from Bernard Baruch and Harry Hopkins to Henry Wallace and Frances Perkins and they brought their expertise, ideas and hope to the administration of the New Deal.

That Franklin Roosevelt had no master plan or unified bureaucratic idea of how to end the depression other than to provide relief to the poor, attempt instigate economic recovery and institute some type of reforms in finance, meant very little to the millions who voted for him. FDR's main asset as a candidate was the hope he inspired at a time in need of hope and inspiration. Anthony Badger's *The New Deal* presents the New Dealers as individuals who followed FDR's basic direction to: do something, try something and if it doesn't work try something else.[1] Looking at the programs, reforms and players of the program, they do not have a shared desire to implement a uniform Progressive bureaucracy as discussed in Weibe, nor are they acting out of any acute "status anxiety." Badger's portraits are those of sober, relatively conservative, individuals looking for an immediate working solution to the crisis. They were *New Dealers.* In a sense Gellhorn was not. She was young, had no work experience or any experience with large corporate groups. She was an idealistic youth raised to believe in her parents Progressivism. Although she did not suffer from status anxiety, she was often acutely aware of the social inequality.[2]

Harry Hopkins was one of the most influential people in the New Deal. Born in 1890 in Sioux City, Iowa, Hopkins attended Grinnell College and graduated in 1912. His father was a harness maker and his mother was a home maker. Hopkins was raised in a Methodist home and steeped in the social gospel by his mother. After his graduation from Grinnell, he launched his career in social work at the Christodoro settlement house on the Lower East Side of New York City. The following year he began working for the New York Association for Improving the Condition of the Poor (AICP). These were formative years for Hopkins. He emerged from the period with strong ideas about work relief versus the dole, and the use of public funds to support mothers with dependent children. Hopkins believed that providing work programs for the unemployed was the best way to deliver relief.[3]

Harry Hopkins background as a New York City social worker led him to the conviction early on that the long term answer for social problems was full-employment. It was a way to ensure economic stability, keep worker morale up and discourage long term dependency, inject money into the economy and in essence to encourage the Protestant work ethic he had grown up with and which pervaded the era. Hopkins came to believe strongly in direct relief support for mothers with children and mothers' pensions and the domestic training for women.[4]

Hopkins' social work background in New York City, his Red Cross work during World War I and his positions with the New York

Tuberculosis Association, along with his eventual appointment to head the New York State relief programs from 1931 until 1933; all led him to his position in Roosevelt Administration as a federal relief administrator. Harry Hopkins oversaw a number of direct programs, like the Federal Writers Project, and other broad programs like the FERA, NIRA and NRA. With the larger more wide reaching programs, there were no mechanisms for the federal government to get relief directly to the people; the solution was to work with states and their relief organizations to get relief where it was needed. There were problems in those systems; local prejudices against relief often dictated who was deemed "worthy" of relief. Race and class origin were also factors. The system was imperfect, but in a very short time a great deal of money was delivered to those in need and that money in turn gave a small boost to the overall economy.

More successful were the large scale federal relief programs which not only improved the infrastructure, but also were a means to get relief money directly to areas in need, be it in Appalachia or central Washington. The breadth of relief programs inserted needed economic stimulus in a way which the federal government had more control over than the state administered relief systems.

As time went on, states formalized bureaucracies and improved implementation of relief funds. The exceptions to this were states like New York with a bureaucracy which grew out of the Progressive reforms already in place. This was Hopkins's and Roosevelt's general model. It is noteworthy that Lyndon Johnson was appointed administrator of the Texas National Youth Administration (TNYA) and his ideas about grass roots level reform came from that personal experience, not from any experience understanding how unwieldy the mechanisms were which allowed for a program like the TNYA to function on a broad scale. The same can be said for Martha Gellhorn, who for a short period was a small cog in the machinery of government. She had no working knowledge of how the mechanisms of the New Deal worked, she just felt it was the right thing at the right time and by virtue of holding a job with the Federal Emergency Relief Agency (FERA) for a short period of time, she felt included as a part of the New Deal. Martha's limited involvement also gave her what she believed was a deep understanding of how the American government functioned.

Gellhorn's version of returning to the US to work for the FERA written in the 1980s is simplified, youthful and heroically tinged with nostalgia:

> It dawned on me that my own country was in trouble. I thought trouble was a European Specialty. America was safe, right and quiet, separate from life around me...I decided to return and offer my services to the nation.[5]

It is easy to visualize Gellhorn's Charis, the juvenile heroine of her first novel, saying the exact same thing.

As it was more often than not, Gellhorn's introduction to Hopkins came through a St. Louis friend Marquis (Mark) Childs.[6] Childs had worked for *The St. Louis Post Dispatch* and became their Washington correspondent in 1934. Childs introduced Gellhorn to Lorena Hickok.

Hickok was Hopkins most trusted and his primary investigator. Her reports alone provide massive front-line first hand observation of the Great Depression and the New Deal. Gellhorn's reports are dwarfed by the sheer number and detail of Hickok's reports. Much of Hickok's collected reports to Hopkins have been reprinted in *One Third of a Nation: Lorena Hickok Reports on the Great Depression*. Of course, so much has been made of Hickok's relationship with Eleanor Roosevelt in recent years that Hickok's greater contribution, the broad detailed documentation of America under the duress of the Great Depression, has been overshadowed.[7]

Hickok arranged a meeting for Gellhorn with Harry Hopkins, director of the FERA, and Gellhorn persuaded him that he should put her journalistic talents to work for him in the FERA.[8] Hopkins was impressed. Gellhorn was over confident, fresh, and inexperienced but her brash attitude and solid social conscience appealed to Hopkins and he appointed her to the lucrative position of Relief-Investigator-at-Large. Gellhorn was provided with a train pass, $5 per day per diem and a salary of $35 per week.[9] This salary, at a time when Harry Hopkins proposed a $1,200 per year per family cap and families on relief were receiving anywhere from $2.50 to $3.50 per week in food vouchers in order to survive, was extraordinary. At the height of the depression, the job was not only exclusive, it was lucrative.[10]

There were a total of sixteen reporters working for Hopkins covering specific regions. Three of them were "at large" investigators and Gellhorn was one of the three. All of his reporters sent and addressed their reports directly to "Dear Mr. Hopkins…" While his reporters were not social workers, Hopkins social work background was reflected in his directions to his relief reports. He was keenly interested in how the Depression and relief were shaping American culture and if a permanent unemployable underclass was being created. He wanted to know if people were being alienated socially and if there was a sense of massive disenfranchisement among the unemployed. Bauman and Cooke note that these themes permeate the FERA reports to Hopkins and that the reports themselves must have affirmed Hopkins belief that "extended joblessness vitiated the human spirit and that direct relief assistance in money and kind, demoralized the recipients."[11] Gellhorn certainly concurred with that assessment.

Gellhorn's acceptance of a job with the FERA might be considered an attempt to redeem herself in her father's eyes. She was returning to the US without de Jouvenel and finally had a real job. This was no mere flitting about earning money freelancing leaning on her St. Louis connections. The FERA was job actually doing something about the situation in America and she wanted to be a part of the New Deal. Gellhorn tackled her new job with the same vigor, enthusiasm and idealism that she brought to every assignment during her life. It is her involvement with the FERA that was the only structured traditional employment she had in her 89 years. It is significant because it is her one and only bout with the Federal Bureaucracy in America, and as well it is her only experience with anything close to a regular job that most people can relate to.

The FERA's most immediate task was to set up a mechanism for dispersing aide and relief to the unemployed. A matching funds situation developed between the federal and state and local governments and in theory the sum was 1:3. The secondary component of the program was one which provided direct grants to individuals and communities to aide with rents, doctor bills and primarily food. As Jacqueline Orsagh noted, "The FERA attempted to keep people alive with a minimum of food and medicine and clothing."[12] As an investigator at large, Gellhorn was assigned the task of getting out into the field and seeing if the programs were working and the funds getting where they most needed to be. Of later and broader lasting importance, the reporting represents that "a chapter in a broader national quest to discover American culture undertaken during the 1930s by writers, social scientist, artist, photographers, playwrights and others."[13]

Moreover, the assignment required brief, but substantive reports from the field to Harry Hopkins very similar to Gellhorn's later war journalism. In these letters to Hopkins, Gellhorn demonstrates her ability to cut through to the most telling aspects of a story. Gellhorn's South Carolina report on November 5, 1934 not only illustrates her hectic routine, but it also revealed the extent that she worked to get a balanced perspective of the relief situation. Visiting a variety of cities and small towns, including Columbia, Greenville, Spartanburg and Rock Hill, she:

> attempted to interview the county administrator, and head social worker, Mill owners, Union presidents, individual social workers, a doctor caring for textile workers, a doctor in charge of the county clinic, relief clients, textile workers; as many of these as possible in their native haunt. Sometimes this list is not complete and sometimes I have added a prominent business man, a mayor, a teacher, and a judge. Within the limits of time (it's all pretty breathless) I have tried to get a check on every point of view noted, by listening to the opposition [sic].[14]

She condemned the local bosses for the high rent they charged in the workers' slums and the inflated grocery prices in the company stores. Also in the South Carolina report, she recreated a scene for Hopkins indicative of the poor health conditions that were prevalent in the country:

> I have seen a village where the latrines drain nicely down a gully to a well from which they get their drinking water. Nobody thinks anything about this; but half the population is both syphilitic and moronic and why they aren't all dead of typhoid I don't know.[15]

Gellhorn is blunt in her concern regarding "unskilled, uneducated laborer… getting use to relief."[16] She is quite candid and unknowingly reveals her inability to transcend her class and class prejudices:[17]

> Half the people I see accept this relief querulously; their only complaint is that a neighbor is getting more. What neighbor I ask; where; how many in his family…no, and what do they care: he's getting more – that's all that counts. And I want it too; gimme; gimme because it is my right; I deserve to be supported (you deserve a job but this world should not be built on charity; should not be built on a few who pay for the many.[18]

Gellhorn continues adding that the newer immigrants seem to be better adept at dealing with the situation in comparison with those more established groups who seemed to be "getting use to relief." This is a bias she will repeat in reports during later forays across the US after World War II.

Gellhorn chose to reprint portions of a twenty four page letter to Harry Hopkins on conditions in *The View From the Ground*. Gellhorn's commentary reflects the social values she maintained and mirrored much of what she wrote about in *The Trouble I've Seen*. However in *The View from the Ground,* in her reprinted reports to Harry Hopkins, she is far more direct and matter of fact in her commentary, than in *The Trouble I've Seen*. She seems to hold out little hope for the poor:

> Health: the Welfare nurses, doctors, social workers, the whole band, tell me that t.b. is on the increase. Naturally; undernourishment is the best guarantee known for bum lungs. The children have impetigo—as far as I can make out

dirt has a lot to do with this. Rickets, anemia, bad teeth, flabby muscles...

Another bright thought: feeblemindedness is on the increase. Doctors speak of these people as being in direct degeneration from parent to child. My own limited experience is this: out of every three families I visited one had moronic children or one moronic parent. I don't mean merely stupid; I mean definitely below normal level intelligence, fit only for sanitariums.[19]

Gellhorn is even blunter in her description of venereal disease of epic proportions, the lack of educated health officials and the use of home made cures for V.D. It is clear that Gellhorn leaned toward a program of eugenics, along the lines of Margaret Sanger and other progressive reformers. Gellhorn did not promote a racist/racial eugenics agenda at all, but was appalled at the situation she saw. Whether it is because she was the daughter and granddaughter of two leading gynecologists of their day or just because it made sense to attempt to relieve some of suffering she saw among the masses, Gellhorn's tone toward sterilization and birth control is clear. She was appalled at the refusal of health officials to sign "sterilization warrants on imbeciles" with the health official maintaining it "was a man's prerogative to have children." Continuing she writes of the V.D clinics she saw and the clinic doctors who usually only saw patients in the late and incurable stages of the disease and after the whole family had been infected:

Congenital syphilis is a terrible problem and practically untreated; nature kills off these children pretty well. One doctor whose clientele was entirely millworkers showed me 50 Wassermans, 5 all four plus. Not one of those people is taking treatment. All of them have families. As you know, these people sleep four in a bed; with the smallest children in the same bed with the parents. Cases: a woman brought in a four-month-old baby; both of them looked deathly ill and the child was paralyzed. The mother thought it was infantile; they were both four plus Wassermans. But the treatment costs 25 cents a shot, and in that area the clinic is not allowed to accept relief orders for treatment; they were not being treated. . . . Saw a family of four; everyone has syphilis. The boy was moronic; and the girl also had t.b. ... A twelve-year-old girl with open syphilitic sores; her mother thought she had scratched a bite which had become infected.[20]

Gellhorn's tone is paternalistic and elitist. She continues and blends the problem of race and disease:

But amongst the Negroes syphilis is "rheumatism." And amongst the ignorant mill workers it is "bad blood." In neither case can any adequate job be done; partly because the people themselves are ignorant and careless. The doctors tell me that they have one child a year born to syphilitics, just as nicely as to the others.[21]

That in the late 1980s, Gellhorn chose to reprint these reports reinforces that Gellhorn's position had not appreciably changed her opinions and still held the beliefs of her youth regarding her assessments as an FERA investigator at large. All in all, they could easily be Dr. Gellhorn's observations.

After two months of crisscrossing the country and sending Hopkins in-depth written reports, she became frustrated with the graft and corruption she had witnessed in the administration of the various relief programs. She felt as if her reportage was making no difference at all. As Gellhorn told it, she stormed into Hopkins' office to "resign and write a bitter expose" of the misery she had witnessed.[22] Hopkins, who had been sending Eleanor Roosevelt

copies of her reports, suggested she speak with Mrs. Roosevelt
before quitting. Mrs. Roosevelt, who had to be aware that Martha
was the daughter of Edna Gellhorn, listened to her "tirade" and
suggested that she speak to "Franklin."[23] Thus after a dinner and
private meeting with President Roosevelt, pleading to him the plight
of the poor which had so frustrated her, she was persuaded that the
best thing she could do for the unemployed was to continue working
for the FERA. It is also this event which marked the beginning of
Martha Gellhorn's adult friendship with the Roosevelt's, which
would last until their deaths.[24]

It is noteworthy that Gellhorn's version of the story was
published in 1988, over 50 years after the fact. In it she explains that
she nearly walked out on the Roosevelt's dinner. In her version, she
is brash and naive. She wrote, at the dinner she:

> Observed in glum silence the white and gold china and the
> copious though not gourmet food, hating this table full of
> cheerful well-fed guests. Didn't they know that better people
> were barefoot and in rags and half-starved; didn't they know
> anything about America?[25]

As her account continues, the situation at the dinner table got
worse before it got better. Mrs. Roosevelt "shouted, 'Franklin talk to
that girl. She says all the unemployed have pellagra and syphilis.'"[26]
This comment caused a silence at the table, followed by a round of
laughter and just as Gellhorn was about to storm out of the room, the
President stopped her. President Roosevelt took her aside to a
private office, fixed her a martini and they had a chat. He listened to
what she had to say and in the end convinced Gellhorn that she could
do more good by staying with the job than quitting.[27]

She returned to the field to continue reporting. For just under a year, Gellhorn worked for the FERA, writing numerous reports and compiling information on living and working conditions all over the country. Her reports represent a very conscientious effort on Gellhorn's part to present a balanced and detailed account of the various conditions of the poor and unemployed. The reports still provide a primary view of conditions during the Depression.

Gellhorn's principal area of assignment covered the textile regions of the South and New England, but at least at the end of her career with the FERA, she used her rail pass and credentials to tour the Pacific Northwest with Bertrand de Jouvenel.[28]

De Jouvenel returned to the United States in June of 1935 on the *Normandie* and met with Gellhorn in August.[29] He had hoped to rekindle their relationship, but that was not to happen. However, Gellhorn used her rail pass and FERA status to accompany him on his travels. They were in Moscow, Idaho, by the last week of August visiting the headquarters of Frank Robinson's *Psychiana* -- a new religion of psychology, which sold the idea of hope and encompassed "the ideals of rising American modernism."[30] It was from there that Gellhorn left to go to Coeur d'Alene where an incident with workers ended her civil service career.

Gellhorn's civil service career was short lived, in spite of her friendship with the Roosevelts. She wrote to her parents:

> I am out of this man's government because I'm a 'dangerous Communist' and the Department of Justice believes me to be a menace...seems the unemployed go about quoting me and refuse--after my visits--to take things lying down.[31]

By her own account, in Coeur d'Alene, Idaho, she met a group of unemployed who were being exploited by corrupt contractors. As Gellhorn remembered it, "By buying beer and haranguing them, I convinced a few hesitant men to break the windows of the FERA office at night."[32] Gellhorn urged the group not to stand idly by, but to act to bring attention to the corrupt contractor. This "protest group" later threw rocks at the windows of the relief building. The FBI investigation put an end not only to the corrupt contractor, but also Martha Gellhorn's career with the FERA. In her version, it did not sit very well with the FBI that a relief reporter, who had been very uncooperative in reporting on any organized protest groups, was now out spurring them on.[33]

While it is unlikely that Gellhorn would necessarily fabricate a story of this proportion, it is probable that her account of the situation is highly exaggerated. It is by no means a certainty that she is reporting the truth in this instance. This account was published in *The View From the Ground* in 1988. In that same edition and her narrative of the articles, she is misleading regarding a later account of a lynching published in the *New Republic*. No FBI record remains of the "investigation" or her dismissal. Review of the newspaper archives in Coeur D'Alene shows no coverage of the incident whatsoever. As well while unemployment was still a problem in the area, there were numerous advertised and available jobs in the region for able workers. Had the shovel incident been as acute as Gellhorn portrays it, there were other readily available jobs available for the men.[34] What is likely is that a brash girl chatted up the boys, bought them beer, and they did go out and throw rocks at the Relief Building. This no doubt angered local civil servants and Gellhorn's luxurious job as a relief reporter came to an end.

In her account of the incident in Idaho, she is the brash and committed crusading civil servant and writer. The incident also says much regarding the nature of the relationship between Gellhorn and the Roosevelts. Gellhorn would no more have thought to ask the

Roosevelts to intervene for her in this situation, than the Roosevelts would have thought to intervene for her. Instead, the bureaucracy ran its course and a minor civil servant was terminated. What the Roosevelts did, however, speaks to the nature of their relationship. Gellhorn received a message from the President and "Mrs. R" offering her a place to stay at their house for a while.[35] Eleanor encouraged Martha to write about her experiences and she used her time at the White House to begin the first draft of a collection of stories titled *The Trouble I've Seen.*

It is also during this period of on and off staying at the White House that Gellhorn connects with H.G. Wells. Gellhorn's relationship with Wells is chronicled in Andrea Lynn's *Shadow Lovers: The Last Affairs of H.G. Wells.* What is clear about Gellhorn's relationship with Wells is that the relationship is unclear. Whether they were lovers, as Wells claimed or they were not, as Gellhorn claimed, cannot be proven. What is clear is that Martha was strongly attracted to Wells as a literary figure, and she establishes her pattern of connecting with men of literary clout. Wells was definitely attracted to her. Early on it is Wells' whom she will spend time with, correspond and remain friends until his death in 1943. Later, it will be with the most celebrated author of the century Ernest Hemingway.[36]

---

[1] Gordon Lloyd, Herbert Hoover, and Franklin D. Roosevelt, *The Two Faces of Liberalism: How the Hoover-Roosevelt Debate Shapes the 21st century* (Salem: M&M Scrivener Press, 2006), 75.

[2] While Gellhorn's social conscience is a thread through most of her published works, Gellhorn quotes Hemingway in *Travels with Myself and*

Another saying "M. is going off to take the pulse of the nation." (p.15) Her more private thoughts were at times less about the pulse of the nation and more about her perception of the answers to domestic social problems and personal prejudices. Some of ideas are paternalistic and even border on calling for eugenics programs.

[3] June Hopkins, *Harry Hopkins: Sudden Hero, Brash Reformer*, The Franklin and Eleanor Roosevelt Institute Series on Diplomatic and Economic History (New York: St. Martin's Press, 1999), 3.

[4] Gwendolyn Mink, *The Wages of Motherhood: Inequality in the Welfare State, 1917-1942* (Ithaca, NY: Cornell University Press, 1995), 158.

[5] Gellhorn, *The View from the Ground*, 69.

[6] Robert A. Rabe, "Marquis W. Childs," in *Encyclopedia of American Journalism*, ed. Stephen Vaughn (New York: Routledge, 2008), 95-96.

[7] As for Hickok's alleged sexual relationship with Eleanor Roosevelt, Martha Gellhorn was livid at the assertion that there might have been a sexual liaison between the two. FDR Oral History Project (February 20, 1980). She was equally adamant that there was no liaison in my interview with her on 11 August 1991 in London.

[8] FDR Oral History Project.

[9] Moorehead, *Gellhorn: A Twentieth-Century Life*, 77. Moorehead lists the amount of Gellhorn's pay at $35 per week. In *The View from the Ground*, 69, Gellhorn notes her salary as $75 per week with train voucher and per diem.

[10] The approximate value of $35 in 2011 is $575. This placed Gellhorn at an approximate 2011 salary of $29,000, not including her per diem expenses of $5 per day which equates to approximately $80 in 2011 values. While it does not seem especially lucrative, in light of her lack of education and experience, coupled with the massive unemployment of the depression, Gellhorn was privileged

[11] John F. Bauman and Thomas H. Coode, *In the Eye of the Great Depression: New Deal Reporters and the Agony of the American People* (DeKalb: Northern Illinois University Press, 1988), 191.

[12] Orsagh, "A Critical Biography of Martha Gellhorn," 24.

[13] Bauman and Coode, 191.

[14] Orsagh, "A Critical Biography of Martha Gellhorn," 28.

[15] Ibid.

[16] Ibid., 29.

[17] She writes at a rapid pace, without necessarily paying attention to grammar or usage, but capturing the scene in the flow of her stream of consciousness. This is similar to her later reportage except by that point, she flows, yet consistently pays closer attention to usage.

[18] Gellhorn and Moorehead, *The Collected Letters of Martha Gellhorn*, 30.

[19] Gellhorn, *The View from the Ground*, 20-21; Harry Hopkins Papers, Franklin Delano Roosevelt Library Hyde Park, NY, Box 13.

[20] Ibid., 15.

[21] Ibid.

[22] Ibid., 70.

[23] Ibid.

[24] Ibid.

[25] Ibid., 75.

[26] Ibid.

[27] Ibid.

[28] Rollyson, *Nothing Ever Happens to the Brave*, 75.

[29] National Archives and Records Administration, Immigration Records, Year: *1935*; Arrival: *New York*; Microfilm Serial: *T715*; Microfilm Roll: *T715_5651*; Line: *24*; Page Number: *20*.

[30] Mary Abshire, "Psychiana," http://www.class.uidaho.edu/narrative/theory/psychiana.htm, n.d. accessed 12 December 2010.

---

[31] Gellhorn, *The View from the Ground*, 71.

[32] Ibid.

[33] Ibid.; FDR Oral History Project.

[34] "The Coeur d'Alene Press." Coeur d'Alene, ID, Coeur d'Alene Public Library Collection. A thorough review of newspapers from the period beginning on July 25, 1935 through November 28, 1935 revealed no reported incidents of protest groups, broken windows or FBI investigations.

[35] Gellhorn, *The View from the Ground*, 70-72.

[36] Andrea Lynn, *Shadow Lovers: The Last Affairs of H.G. Wells* (Boulder, Colo.: Westview Press, 2001).Gellhorn during her life made few mentions of her affairs, but she has a pattern of casual sexual relationships with a variety of men, many married, and in positions of power or prestige. In regard to Wells, she denied the affair. He claims they had an affair. Later in life, she became friends with one of Wells' more well known lovers, Rebecca West. When I interviewed Gellhorn in 1991, she gave me a copy of Rebecca West's *The Judge* as a gift.

CHAPTER 4

REALISM AND THE GREAT DEPRESSION

In a conscious attempt to avoid repeating the failure of her first novel, Gellhorn wrote *The Trouble I Have Seen* with a distinct calculated structural purpose. Her point was to show "the four ages of man, the four points of the compass, the exact variety of experiences."[1] She also balances her portraits with two stories dealing primarily with men and the other two dealing with women and works a reverse chronology with the ages of the people in her portraits and their ordering in the book. The oldest character Mrs. Maddison begins the book and the youngest, Ruby, ends the book. As well these are the two strongest sections of the book. This regression highlights effects of the Depression on those who were experiencing it as people who at one time had a relatively secure life, to those men in the midst of life struggling to have relationships, younger men worried over enough money to marry, struggling to keep their jobs, and to a child who prostitutes herself for roller-skates and ice cream because she doesn't know any better.

Gellhorn covered the areas of Hopkins concern regarding the effect of relief on the psyche of the nation. The book served as "a record of failure." Orsagh noted that she worked to "shave away the excess that was largely at fault in her first novel and to imitate the concentration of Hemingway."[2] Gellhorn took direct exception to that statement, probably because of the Hemingway comparison, but Orsagh is correct in her comparative assessment of *The Trouble I've Seen* with *What Mad Pursuit*, The *Trouble I've Seen* was far more powerful because Gellhorn dropped her first person narrative which had been so unsuccessful in *What Mad Pursuit* and began to mesh her third person narrative and her reporter's eye, and in turn create believable characters.

The Trouble I've Seen is Gellhorn's first successful writing endeavor which combines her research and translates that into a realist novel in the tradition of the Progressive realists. In the tradition of Upton Sinclair and *The Jungle*, Gellhorn attempts to couch her reportage in fiction and like Sinclair, her portraits of the individual struggling fade against the pallet of the setting, in Gellhorn's case the Great Depression.[3] While she boldly attempts to focus on the humanity and the individual suffering, her portraits grow fainter and the individuals are absorbed into the background. The story the reader comes away with is one of a portrait of suffering and conditions during the Great Depression, not the human aspect of that suffering.

Gellhorn crosses generational lines in an attempt to show the impact of the economic hardships of the time on more than one age band of individuals, but it is not a work of fiction that explores the internal human condition. Gellhorn's focus is on the concessions individuals have to make to survive, yet those concessions are more reportorial in nature and do not leave the reader with an enriched view of the individual's internal conflicts. The book's greatest success was in that it showed Gellhorn could write a palatable novel, not as a novel in the realist tradition.

However, from the perspective of 2012, the portraits Gellhorn drew clearly illuminate a small part of the effect of the Great Depression. In 1999, Milton Wolff noted that he had purchased Gellhorn's *Novellas* and read the Depression book, but he stated "I don't mean any offense to Martha, but that book is just flat."[4]

Arguably, it is the first three sections of the book which fall flat, but still provide a glimpse of the era.

In its final form, the stories and prose in *The Trouble I've Seen* would have been enough to insure sales, but Gellhorn was aided by two of her more powerful friends. H.G. Wells, with whom Gellhorn had stayed during part of the writing of the book, liked the work well enough to write the introduction. At the time of its publication one reviewer noted that Wells' introduction over stated the significance of the book,

> Though it does not entirely deserve the praise which H.G. Wells accords it in his preface, Miss Gellhorn's second book is startlingly superior to her first"[5]

The *New Republic's* assessment was also positive:

> Anyone with the slightest understanding in the relief situation will agree that no story in Miss Gellhorn's book is typical…there is a human reality about all the stories…at the core of each there is a pattern of reality that is of wide enough significance to take the out of the class of the eccentric…the abominable cruelty, short-sightedness and general all-around social imbecility of those who defame the relief recipients *en mass* will be thoroughly exposed.[6]

Mrs. Roosevelt gave the book a glowing review in her 'My Day" Column.[7] As well Mrs. Roosevelt provided a quote for the dust jacket, "A very remarkable piece of writing…she can make many people and situations real for us…"[8]

The Trouble I've Seen, uses very clear and realistic portraits of believable individuals, personalized the poverty and distress occurring all over the country. *The Trouble I've Seen* attempts to weave in it Harry Hopkins areas of special interest into the "role of

the depression and relief in shaping American culture."[9] Although
the book follows closely proletarian realism, the call to revolution is
missing. Written independently from any primary ideological
message, it is Gellhorn's straight-from-the-heart, honest appraisal of
the situation. *The Trouble I've Seen* did not become a classic. At its
best, it endures as a work which defines a portion of the many
Depression experiences. Gellhorn noted that "fiction was infinitely
more interesting than journalism" and that it was a process of
looking at the big picture and "getting it from big to small." By
those definitions, *The Trouble I've Seen* is an important progression
for Gellhorn as a writer.[10]

The first section of the book *Mrs. Maddison* is the story of an
older woman, once secure, now learning to balance her pride with
her newly found impoverished situation. In Martha's words:

> We all had it better once, Mrs. Maddison decided. We were
> real folks once we had placed to live, we had families, and
> we knew what we'd be doing the next year and the next one.
> Now, now…A familiar feeling of uncertainty overcame Mrs.
> Maddison a fear that everything would blow away even as
> she waited' things would change once attain, there wouldn't'
> even be this piddling work for her, this measly living.[11]

Mrs. Maddison's family is her life and they are all struggling with
the same dilemma, but reacting in various ways to the stress –
alcoholism, domestic violence and rebellion. Mrs. Maddison's
primary purpose is to make sure her granddaughter "Tiny" gets
enough to eat and survives the economic situation. She struggles,
works any job available, pinches pennies. She leaps at the
opportunity to move from the city to the countryside in hopes of a
chance to at least be able to earn a basic living.

On the farm, she winds up in a "Negro sharecropper's" cabin and her hopes again are crushed.[12] The situation on the farm also serves to demonstrate in human terms the time it takes to resolve the economic crisis. Mrs. Maddison's hopes are shattered as the relief she envisioned, a fruitful life in the country, is not to be and she has basically sunk to the life of a failed sharecropper. The situation seems hopeless, with no end in sight, and while she hangs on, her family disintegrates into the despair of the situation. Gellhorn sinks into sentimentality with a contrived ending finishing the story of Mrs. Maddison with the woman picking up a pencil and writing a long letter to Mr. Roosevelt.

The second section of Gellhorn's novel deals with *Joe and Pete,* two workers involved with their union and a strike. Joe, the intellectual union organizer who has inspired the trust and admiration of his men, calls a halt to a three day strike after realizing the futility of the effort. The scabs are retained and Joe's workers are laid off.

Pete, one of those workers who had been able to keep himself and his family in more or less middle class circumstances, finds himself out of work with no real hope of employment. Pete believed in the system and tries and tries again to find a job, but is finally reduced to selling shoe strings and gum on a street corner. At one point, Pete saw a competitor and rushes to crush his competition and in the process realizes the competitor is a blind man. Pete is crushed, his manhood and his faith lost. At the end of the story, Joe is asked by his men to resign from his union position. In a last futile attempt to strike out at the factory, Joe approaches the factory with a brick in hand, but drops it and then heads to the freight yard to bum a ride off into the distant nowhere that encompasses the country.

Jim Comes Home, the third installment is a story about a man whose family is torn apart by poverty. It is the most melodramatic of the selections in the book and in the single story Gellhorn runs the gamut of the Depression with Jim and his family. Jim is younger than Joe and Pete and has been working on a farm for six weeks. He decides to return home. Walking the path to his house, he hears his father and sister battling over who she goes out with and how late she stays out. Jim at twenty returns to school with his sister because he has no work or anything better to do, and he has a dream of becoming a doctor. He is quickly frustrated, he is older and he is different, and reality overwhelms his dreams.

Jim finds himself in a bar with an old friend who is now working in the mines. His friend shares the fear, the hopelessness and despair he feels in the mines. A few hours later as Jim and his friend leave the bar drunk, Jim is hit by a truck. He winds up in the hospital, the place he dreams of belonging. The intern is kind and let's Jim watch a surgery. Later Jim's sister is pregnant, his father is livid and mother sinks into a dissociative state and is hospitalized. In the second portion of Jim's story, he meets Lou and falls in love. They eventually marry and in clothes Jim stole for the occasion.

In many ways, *Jim* is just a continuation of *Joe and Pete* and the male perspective of the Depression. The men in the stories present the reader with individuals who are trending toward, if not already at the point of, social alienation. Throughout both sections, Gellhorn peppers a variety and breadth of the stories of men. It is in the portrait of working men that Gellhorn falls short and into sentimental cliché and quick simplistic endings.

The final story in *The Trouble I've Seen* is the most difficult for the reader and demonstrates the despair of the Depression in a manner that cannot be ignored or easily forgotten. Many of Gellhorn's reports to Harry Hopkins dealt with the issue of child prostitution. In her report of 25 August 1935 from Camden, New Jersey, Gellhorn wrote Hopkins that:

> It appears that the depression is resulting in a lot of amateur prostitution…the age limit is going down and unmarried mothers are very young. …I've seen the girls. Obviously, they want clothes, and a little fun. It's grim to think what they are getting for their trouble.[13]

Ruby deals with this issue graphically and is Gellhorn's best effort in *The Trouble I've Seen.*

Ruby is the story of an eleven year old girl who becomes a prostitute initially in order to get toothpaste to go with the prize of a toothbrush. Ruby is lured into a ring of thirteen year old prostitutes by the promise of simple children's things, like an ice cream cone now and then or a pair of skates. For thirty cents a day, Ruby becomes a prostitute. It would have been easy for Gellhorn to have just told Ruby's story, but in a deft maneuver she is able to give the reader a glimpse at the men who frequent these young prostitutes and the mixed emotions and despair that they feel. As noted in the review of The Trouble I've Seen in *The Nation*, "the child's tragedy is all together pitiful and convincing."[14] Yet, Gellhorn is unable to create any meaningful internal dialogue and missed the opportunity to take the story to the next level

Grace Lumpkin's *To Make My Bread* offers the closest point of comparison to contextualize Gellhorn's work roughly within its time period. Gellhorn was allowed access to travel nationwide while working with the FERA, but her primary assignment area was the mill towns of the South, the setting of Lumpkin's work. Published in 1932, four years before Gellhorn's book, *To Make My Bread* centers on life in Appalachia and the exodus from the hills to the mills, along with the internal dialogue and personal narrative that

brings the plight of her characters to life. The book concludes with a
narrative of the Loray Mill Strike. It was a boldly political work and
demonstrated the intricacies of the union and of a major strike in a
far more poignant manner than Gellhorn. And, like Gellhorn,
Lumpkin crosses age bands to give a multi-generational facet to her
story. The portraits and story by Lumpkin hold up more strongly
today than Gellhorn's do. As A.O. Scott noted in a review in *The
Nation* in 1996:

> Lumpkin's narrative is in places flawed, in others forced; but
> this novel is an honest, clear eyed and coherent attempt to make
> sense of the enormities of social change as they manifest
> themselves in the lives of individuals.[15]

Gellhorn fell short in her portrayal of the internal conflict and
growth of the characters, and she did not attempt to strike upon any
deeper feminist themes as did Lumpkin's work. Gellhorn's heroines
fall far short of Lumpkin's Emma and Bonnie.[16]

Some of Gellhorn's liberal attitudes and later affiliations would
cause more right-wing reactionaries to label her a "fellow traveler."
It must be noted that although Gellhorn's attitudes were liberal, and
even with the run in with the FBI in Coeur D'Alene and her later
affiliation with the *causa* of the Spanish Republic, she was not a
communist. In essence she was too middle class by nature to be a
communist; she was however a member of the small group of writers
who managed to transcend the radical "Left/Right" party
polarizations of the 1930s. Although *The Trouble I've Seen* follows
closely proletarian realism, one important aspect--the call to
revolution--is missing. Both Edith Walton and Dorothy Thompson
noted this fact in their reviews. Walton recognizes this as she
praised Gellhorn:

> She writes well; she is not patronizing; her insight for an outsider is compassionate and shrewd. There is room in her book for a stronger note of protest…[17]

Unlike Lumpkin, Gellhorn's book was written independently from any primary ideological message, and stands as a straight-from-the-heart, honest appraisal of the situation, with a message that came across rather flat. If a socio-political classification is need for the book, it is obviously a view of the Depression from a liberal Rooseveltian bend. It endures as a book which "forcefully defined Depression America."[18]

In Orsagh's assessment of *The Trouble I've Seen* she also observes that while Gellhorn's book closely follows proletarian realism, the call for action is missing. She noted:

> Gellhorn was far too egoistic to spread the "party line," or write propaganda and, more often than not, her favorite characters were middle class persons dismissed from their jobs, not proletarians. Gellhorn never bowed to the spreading of anyone else's message and it was not that crucial aspect of proletarian realism which accounted for the book's failure to endure. The paring down of style, however, until even the beauty is lost, and the topical nature of her subject were serious liabilities.[19]

The Trouble I've Seen is a better book than *What Mad Pursuit* and foreshadows Gellhorn's later efforts blending journalism and fiction and fiction and journalism. The distance of the author from the subject, as well as a conscious effort to write a book that represented the Depression, set the work apart from the narcissistic juvenilia of *What Mad Pursuit*. Also, considering the harshness and bluntness in her letters to Hopkins, Gellhorn's ability to soften her portraits of relief recipients and make the reader empathize with her characters in *The Trouble I've Seen* shows a glimpse of Gellhorn's true talent for realism which will be realized in its fullest in her World War II reportage.

Unfortunately, Gellhorn's father did not live to see the book in print, having unexpectedly died in January of 1935; he did have a chance to read the book.[20] Orsagh notes, "If she had ever dreamed of a best selling book which would launch her name and career, that dream materialized with TTIS."[21] While Gellhorn claims that was not what she was looking for during the period, it is an assertion which is hard to believe considering how much time and effort she had put in to becoming a successful novelist. Her disclaimer that she was "hardly a star figure" flies in the face of her glamorous publicity shots and the carefully cultivated early image of Martha Gellhorn.[22]

The Trouble I've Seen was mature and serious, the antithesis of her first novel. Because it was such an improvement over her first novel, it received generally good reviews. Gellhorn is praised for raising her subjects above the "angle of graphs, charts, or leeches on Relief" and creating a human portrait of the struggles of the Depression.[23] The immediate reviews do not see Gellhorn's sentimentality and the contrived nature of the situation of her characters. To the contrary, the New Republic review actually compliments her for "lavish(ing) on them a sympathy that engages the reader as a partisan of the unfortunates."[24]

Moreover, Gellhorn was bold enough to add a twist to this set of stories. As Jacqueline Orsagh noted:

> Most of us have been aesthetically conditioned by literature and fairy tales to believe in an equalizing process. We expect [these] terribly desperate [stories] a tragedy over which the protagonist triumphs finally, to live happily ever after. A great reward must eventually compensate the character for

his/her great suffering. Here, however, the author's point is that reality lies in another direction. There is no recompense, no happy ending, and the character's goodness is irrelevant. The most to be gleaned from existence is a momentary security.[25]

This realism and lack of sentimentality is even more obviously reflected in Gellhorn's later journalism and war reportage. The essence of the Gellhorn's message is clear and it provides a contrast from the pulp fiction and Busby Berkeley musicals that constituted such a large part of American popular culture of the time. At the same time, it is not as poignant or radical as Lumpkin, but is a great progression for Gellhorn.

After the publication of *The Trouble I've Seen*, Gellhorn left for Europe and tentatively began working on a novel dealing with the rise of Fascism in Europe. The novel did not go well and her attention was easily diverted. Gellhorn was unable to translate her experience with fascism in Europe in to a novel, but she continued to struggle with the project until she finally gave up in early 1937. Her longtime friend from her St. Louis days, Allen Grover read the draft and felt "it read more like a political tract than fiction."[26] The remnants of the novel are in the Gellhorn collection at Boston University and closed to researchers until 2023.[27]

---

[1] Gellhorn, "Notations on *A Critical Biography of Martha Gellhorn* by Jacqueline Elizabeth Orsagh," 54.

[2] Orsagh, *A Critical Biography of Martha Gellhorn*, 54-55.

[3] Harold Bloom, *Upton Sinclair's The Jungle* (New York: Chelsea House Publishers, 2002), 1.

[4] Milton Wolff, August 20-26, 1999; Martha Gellhorn, *The Novellas of Martha Gellhorn*, 1st American ed. (New York: Knopf, 1993).

[5] "Four Panels Illustrate Martha Gellhorn's Theme," *The New York Times* 27 September 1936.

[6] C. Hartley Grattan, "Behind the Figures," *The New Republic* (21 October 1936): 328.

[7] Martha Gellhorn, *The Trouble I've Seen* (New York: William Morrow and Company, 1936).

[8] As quoted in Orsagh, "A Critical Biography of Martha Gellhorn," 51.

[9] Bauman and Coode, 14.

[10] Nigel Forde, "Martha Gellhorn: The Difference Between Fiction and Reporting," in *Bookshelf* (BBC 4 January 1990).

[11] Martha Gellhorn, *The Novellas of Martha Gellhorn*, 1st American ed. (New York: Knopf, 1993), 8.

[12] Ibid., 22.
[13] Letter to Harry Hopkins, Camden NJ, 25 April 25 1935.

[14] Dorothy Van Doren, "Shorter Notices," *Nation* 143, No. 18 (1936).

[15] A. O. Scott, "When We Read Red," *Nation*, 263, No. 8, (1996).

[16] Grace Lumpkin, *To Make My Bread*. The Radical Novel Reconsidered (Urbana: University of Illinois Press, 1995).

[17] Van Doran.

[18] Orsagh, *A Critical Biography of Martha Gellhorn*, 54-55.

[19] Ibid., 55. It is noteworthy that when Gellhorn read Orsagh, she made no comment on this specific assessment of her egotism. She did however take exception, stating "She has inflated everything in this first section, I was hardly a star figure – not!" It is as if Gellhorn read the section she referred to, but was unable to process the gist of what Orsagh was saying because

she was too caught up in worrying about how she came across physically in Orsagh's prose.

[20] Gellhorn and Moorehead, *The Collected Letters of Martha Gellhorn*, 36.

[21] Orsagh, *A Critical Biography of Martha Gellhorn*, 55.

[22] Gellhorn, "Notations on *A Critical Biography of Martha Gellhorn* by Jacqueline Elizabeth Orsagh," 55. Also, nearly all photos printed of Gellhorn with the publicity for *What Mad Pursuit* and *The Trouble I've Seen* are glamour shots and there is a pattern of showing Gellhorn as an alluring woman.

[23] Lawrence Blair, *Survey Graphic* (December 1936): 684.

[24] Grattan, "Behind the Figures."

[25] Orsagh, *A Critical Biography of Martha Gellhorn*, 45.

[26] Gellhorn and Moorehead, *The Collected Letters of Martha Gellhorn*, 49.

[27] The limited exception to that rule granted by the Gellhorn estate to Carolyn Moorehead in order for her to write her biography of Gellhorn and edit her letters. As well Moorehead, allowed Kate McLoughlin access for her work *Martha Gellhorn: The War Writer in the Field and in the Text*.

CHAPTER 5

THE EDUCATION OF A CORRESPONDENT

The Civil War in Spain began in July of 1936 and ended just before the beginning of World War II in April 1939. Internal political strife had been going on far longer. Spain had been in political turmoil since the middle of the 19th century. From its beginning, Spain's forays in to democracy were mired by internal class and religious issues. The first Republic lasted from February of 1873 through December of 1874, just short of two years before the Restoration of the monarchy. However, Spain muddled along in turmoil. At the turn of the 20th century, Catalonian nationalism made Barcelona "the most turbulent city in Europe; the city of bombs."[1] Problems with Catalonians began before the First Republic, had continued and were intensified by Spain's loss of colonial empire.

While there were forays in to Morocco to regain imperial territory, the 1895 Cuban War turned into the 1898, Spanish American War and marked the end of what had been the unparallel empire of Spain. The last remnant of the greatness which had been Imperial Spain was gone. Spain, itself, was torn between trouble with Catalonia, divisions between Carlists, labor unions, anarchists, and all of this sat at an impasse of class division. These mitigating factors were in place prior to the establishment of the Second Republic.[2]

The situation in Spain was complex. Spain's culture was homogeneous and while there was international intervention in Spain, primarily it was a Civil War. Spain was not going to become part of the Third Reich, nor part of an imagined new Fascist Roman Empire. Which group of Spaniards would lead Spain and what type of government Spain would have was what was at stake. With the exception of Basque separatism, since the Inquisition in the 1500s, Catholicism and the Castilians dominated the culture. There would be no great departure from that cultural axis and Spain would rule itself.

In essence, the question was: who was strong enough to unify enough of the populace to rule Spain? In that sense, the Republic was dead on arrival, they lacked experienced cohesive leadership and a populace educated enough to tread water long enough for the Republic to take root. It came down to whether there would be a right wing restoration of the throne or a timelier trend toward a fascist government.

Gellhorn naively compared the situation in Spain to the "Balkans of 1912."[3] It was a different situation completely. The Balkans sat as a historically festering region with long standing multi ethnic and multicultural differences and conflicts, making the Balkan Wars more about the re-division of a contested complicated imperial geopolitical problem. The conflict in Spain was a civil war in nature with geopolitical implications, a rudimentary version of post-World War II conflicts with larger powers interceding in civil wars to further their global geopolitical goals. For Gellhorn, as for many others however, it was a purely anti-fascist war. As well, those like Gellhorn were never completely able to reconcile the post-World War II period because of their ideological bend and naïveté in the face of Cold War realities.

Spain was many things, but it was truly Gellhorn's education as a war correspondent.[4] Spain was the finishing school to her apprenticeship as a writer. After the war in Spain, Gellhorn was a full fledged foreign correspondent. She would no longer rely wholly on friends or connections for work. She stood on her own as a writer. While she remained lesser known that Margaret Bourke-White or Ernie Pyle, Gellhorn's route to her place in their company and her place in popular culture began in Spain.

From the beginning in Madrid, her best work came when she lost herself and became absorbed in moment. Describing herself as a tape recorder with eyes, it was in that mode in which Gellhorn as a writer surpassed herself and set the bar high for others to follow.[5] The magnitude of the moments shrunk Gellhorn's personage, and amplified her unique voice. Each international disaster honed her skills further. From Spain, her voice and story telling skills strengthened and eventually reached their peak during the final year and a half of World War II.[6]

Any discussion of Gellhorn's life inevitably leads to a comparison of her body of work to that of Ernest Hemingway. All too often the comparison dwells on the personal or the superficially literary. Little critical attention has been directed toward a comparative analysis of the work each writer produced during the period as war correspondents. The fact is that from the time Gellhorn and Hemingway fell in love during the Spanish Civil War in 1937, to the collapse of their marriage in the wake of the liberation of France, they were both working as war correspondents, as well as novelists. The pursuit of war – and of each other – shaped their memorable coupling from beginning to a bitter end.

For Hemingway, the attraction to Gellhorn was immediate and overwhelming. She was "his female ideal...the flip side of the same coin."[7] But by the time Gellhorn and Hemingway were married in 1940, they had both gotten to know each other not only as passionate lovers but also as professional writers and strong individualistic personalities. The attraction and antagonism between the bright, virile, and very masculine symbol of the Lost Generation, and a younger woman whose endeavors placed her at the heart of interwar liberalism created a romance and a conflict of legendary proportions.

Hemingway the veteran, the divorced man, the child of a dysfunctional family, arguably spent most of his life searching for the ideal woman to gratify his idealized manhood. It has been said that Hemingway found his perfect mate in Gellhorn, but perhaps he found more than he bargained for.[8] Gellhorn, the brash, attractive child of American Progressivism proved to be something other than an all-affirming helpmate. She wanted much more than a room of her own; she arguably wanted a world of her own outside of Papa Hemingway's orbit. She had always wanted not only to travel the world, but to understand it and to change it for the better.

Gellhorn's introduction to Hemingway and her eventual route to Spain began with an opportune visit to Key West. On the first Christmas holiday after the death of her father, Gellhorn, her mother and younger brother went on a vacation. In December of 1936, the Gellhorns were in Key West. At the time Key West was home base for Ernest Hemingway. When he was not writing, he spent a great deal of his time fishing and drinking at his favorite bar, Sloppy Joe's.

When Gellhorn entered Sloppy Joe's bar that December, she met the most interesting, irresistible, and ultimately infuriating person she would ever know, Ernest Hemingway. Their mutual attraction at first found itself subsumed by Gellhorn's awe at being in the presence of one of her literary heroes. Hemingway was no aging H.G. Wells, he was at his masculine prime. In early January 1937, she wrote Mrs. Roosevelt admiringly about the "fine stories" he told her: "In a writer this is imagination, in anyone else it's lying. That's where genius comes in."[9] In that same letter, she continues with her praise of Hemingway and his advice to her as a writer. It is clear that Hemingway found her attractive, but also viewed her as somewhat of an apprentice writer and himself as the master.

It is a far cry from her earlier assessment of Hemingway in a letter to de Jouvenel bragging that the skiing story in *In Our Times* was about her "ex-beau" and "Hemingway makes him inarticulate simply because Hemingway doesn't know how to talk…Anyway, Hemingway has affected my style which is really too bad; but there you are."[10] His inability to talk was not evident in their first meeting. While both Leicester Hemingway and James McLendon's account of that meeting had Gellhorn alone with Hemingway for the majority of the time, Gellhorn's counters their account of that first meeting. She used that particular situation as "an example of how apocryphal stories grow. I was with my mother and brother and obviously did not leave them."[11]

It was a crossing of paths that proved timely for both writers. Gellhorn was a politically idealistic, less experienced, enthusiastic writer with a penchant for connecting with important people of her time. Hemingway was restless, more experienced; the most established and well known novelist of his generation. What Gellhorn and Hemingway had in common, beyond her awe of him as a writer, was a shared interest and belief in the importance of the war in Spain. She wrote Eleanor Roosevelt of the impending doom:

> If that madman Hitler really sends two divisions to Spain my bet is that war is nearer than even the pessimist's thought. It is horrible to think of Germany just this side of food riots and that maniac…being able to lead a perfectly good nation into something which will finish them up nicely.[12]

Gellhorn returned to St. Louis. She wrote glowingly of her visit to Key West to Ernest's wife Pauline Hemingway. Key West was quite a contrast to the smoky polluted blackout days in St. Louis, where Gellhorn made slow progress on the "peace book" which she abandoned after she left St. Louis for Spain.[13] She wrote fondly of de Jouvenel and sent Pauline two photographs of Bertrand and wrote of a trip to Arcachon she had taken with Bertrand, his wife Marcelle and Marcelle's lover, describing the situation like "a bad farce on the Boulevards."[14] It would be Pauline's husband she would take up with this time, not Marcelle's.

Gellhorn's account of Spain, along with her articles from the war, gives insight into the route she took to become a war correspondent. She had two books under her belt, one successful, one embarrassingly unsuccessful, a draft of an aborted third book which she did not publish, and a relatively successful career as a freelance writer, albeit primarily with her home town newspaper *The St. Louis Post Dispatch*. Her motivation to go to the war in Spain transcended her interest in Ernest Hemingway. At the same time, her connection to Hemingway was extremely helpful. He provided her with access to a place to stay, she accompanied him to the front via car and he had an almost unlimited amount of gas which meant the freedom to move around the fronts in a manner she would never have been able to alone.

While Herbert Matthews of *The New York Times* also served as a mentor, it is clear that Hemingway had the greatest influence on Gellhorn's writing. Hemingway's journalism from the 1920s and early 1930s carried his distinctive rhythm and tone. Arguably, Gellhorn adopted or wrote with a very similar clear rhyme and tone. Not to specifically imply that she overtly copied Hemingway's style, but regardless of his influence or non-influence, there is a very similar resonance. Comparisons between the reportage of the two from Spain provide interesting parallels. For Hemingway, Spain, and to a certain extent in his reports from China, will be the last time Hemingway's war correspondence is more about the wars and what is happening on the front and less about Hemingway's role in what is happening around him.

In Spain, he uses his clear declarative tone and while the reader knows he is there, and he writes from the first person, he is not the primary actor in these articles. It is in this area and at this time, at the beginning of their personal relationship that their writing style seems the most similar in construction and tone. Gellhorn continues to develop her voice as the impassioned observer, while Hemingway diverges from dispassionate observer to the role of crusading, soldier journalist, involved in the fight, winning the war single handedly in the first person from D-Day to the Siegfried line.

However, at this point during the war in Spain, Hemingway was able to temper his desire to be perceived at a military authority. *For Whom the Bell Tolls* is a story about man on a military mission, but Hemingway's tone is balanced and realistic within the character he creates of Robert Jordan's. Hemingway used the heroic professor soldier Robert Merriman, commander of the Abraham Lincoln Brigade's to base Robert Jordon on.[15] With a basis in fact to anchor him, Hemingway was able to combine his love of military tactics and discussion into his characters realistically. *For Whom the Bell Tolls* is his masterwork from the period, his war novel from Spain. He dedicated the novel to Martha Gellhorn and it is clear that there was a great deal of love and adoration for Gellhorn.[16]

In late March 1937, Hemingway was deeply enamored of his protégé, Gellhorn, and his role as her teacher. Gellhorn followed Matthews and Hemingway around Spain and learned about the war firsthand.[17] Ensconced in the Hotel Florida with Hemingway and an assortment of other journalists and war tourists, the hotel and Chicote's Bar nearby were abuzz with activity. Milton Wolfe remembered Chicote's as a place to enjoy his breaks from the front with beautiful young women to keep him company. The Madrid that Gellhorn was plunked into was abuzz with intrigue, heroism, and ego playing against a background of righteous war, all serving to make it somewhat of a surreal atmosphere.[18]

Gellhorn had an unparalleled access to the front thanks to Hemingway, Matthews and Dutch filmmaker Joris Ivans. No other young unproven female journalist could come as close to the front line as easily or as regularly as she did. Gellhorn had access specifically because of her relationship with Hemingway. In the midst of this, Hemingway took on a role he loved, as expert and teacher. He tutored Gellhorn in the finer points of war, helping her learn to hear the difference between incoming and outgoing shells and bullets, instructing her in the finer points of tactics and operations. Gellhorn was Hemingway's trophy. Being able to instructor her in the ways of war and her writing heightened his enjoyment of the war. At the same time, he was contributing money for ambulances and creating positive attention for the *causa,* he was enjoying himself immensely.[19] After being in Madrid with Gellhorn for three weeks, Hemingway asked Gellhorn to marry him.[20]

For Martha, getting to the Civil War was of overwhelming importance, Spain was the place to stop Fascism. This was it. It was one of those moments in history when there was no doubt, and nothing would stop her from being there to witness the struggle.[21] Although Gellhorn had published two books and had a fairly extensive free-lance career, she was neither a foreign correspondent nor a war correspondent. With no credentials or contract, entry into Spain was not a simple task. She did not want to lean on her connection to the Roosevelts for a favor. Instead, she used a St. Louis connection working at *Collier's;* Kyle Crichton wrote a letter on the magazine's letterhead stating she worked for them.

By this point Gellhorn had completely abandoned any pacifist sentiments and had become staunchly anti-fascist.[22] Because she lacked any actual affiliation with a newspaper or magazine, and because of the non-intervention policy, "the French fonctionaire (sic)...a certified brute," refused Gellhorn's request for a visa categorically.[23] The letter from *Colliers* did not impress him and she quickly gave up on the notion of obtaining a visa and entering Spain officially. She proceeded to the Andorran border, and hiked into the country – repeating a journey she had made in the early 1930s and wrote about in *What Mad Pursuit*. She proceeded to walk into Spain, making her way to Madrid via Barcelona. She joined Hemingway who was reporting for the North American News Alliance (NANA) in Madrid.

Gellhorn made her way to the Florida Hotel in Madrid, and met with Hemingway and his entourage in the middle of March 1937.[24] The Florida was "the press mess," the home of the Pro-Republican press corps and Gellhorn's residence during her trips to Madrid.[25] Of the many accounts of that time period in Madrid, Gellhorn noted that Virginia Cowles description of Madrid in *Looking for Trouble* was the closest to being a "more or less accurate description."[26] Gellhorn took great exception to Leicester Hemingway's account of Spain and in general. In particular, she refutes his claim that she and Hemingway "often blended an idea from one with the style of the other and entered the finished product in a magazine under either of their names."[27] In her notes on Jacqueline Orsagh, she wrote "lying must run in the Hemingway family" and viewed Leicester as "maybe no. 1 apocryphiar (sic)."[28]

Virginia Cowles was two years Gellhorn's junior. She published in *Collier's* in the early 1930s and went to cover Spain for the *Sunday Times*. Her first entry into Spain was one week after the battle of Guadalajara in March 1937.[29] This places her and Gellhorn arriving at approximately the same time in Madrid. Cowles arrived in Spain via official channels and on Air France. Unlike Gellhorn, she was employed by the *Sunday Times* and was an actual bona fide foreign correspondent, albeit a junior one.

While Cowles' trip on the surface does not seem as harrowing as Gellhorn's, it was not simple either. She landed in Valencia and had to make her way overland 223 miles to Madrid. Cowles' journey overland was with an American woman propagandist, who had found herself in Spain via Moscow and *The Moscow Daily News,* and a Pro-Republican Priest. They travelled overland, endured detours, check points and roads under fire.[30] While Gellhorn's entre into the country, slipping across the border and hitch hiking to Barcelona made for a slightly more romantic story, Gellhorn's trip from Barcelona to Madrid was via train and made for a smooth crossing of the 450 miles. Gellhorn and Cowles arrival coincided and they both were residents of the Hotel Florida, and from there became life long friends.[31]

The Florida was peppered with a who's who of war correspondents, war tourists and politicos. In addition to Gellhorn and Cowles, there were a number of women, their age and older, residents of varying notoriety. Both Dorothy Parker and Lillian Hellman were temporary residents of the Florida, as well as Josie Herbst. Herbst and Parker both were born in the 19th century. Hellman was just three years Gellhorn's senior and five years older than Cowles. It is easy to be misled into thinking that Gellhorn was one of a few women in Madrid. It is also misleading to think of her as the youngest of the lot of women who found themselves in

Madrid. The aforementioned are just the high profile names. Women with a passion for the *causa* flooded into Spain from all over the world filling a variety of roles from war correspondent, to ambulance drivers and nurses.[32]

Gellhorn's presence created a certain amount of tension due to Hemingway's possessiveness and attachment to her. Milt Wolfe recalled a quick run in with the two of them and Hemingway posturing and taking issue with Wolff trying to take "his girl."[33] In another incident, Hemingway went so far as to challenge Republican General Juan Modesto to a duel over Martha. Orsagh noted that "a General Modesto was also in love with Martha Gellhorn and made three passes at her in front of Hemingway."[34] Gellhorn's comments about the scenario are revealing. She corrected Orsagh, noting that Modesto was "the most famous" General and at the same time notes the whole situation was overblown by Hemingway.[35] Gellhorn's correction to Orsagh in 1989, demonstrates a pattern that recurs with Gellhorn regarding her biography. Gellhorn is revolted by the intrusion into her personal life, and on one hand she plays down the comment and at the same time she revises the information in the end making it clear to a younger generation that not only was he a General, he was one of the most famous.

Another overblown and much repeated example from Spain was a story about Gellhorn not pulling the blinds during a blackout and coming home to a "neat round bullet hole in her hotel window." Gellhorn called the incident "rubbish" and noted "I think this lie stems from E.H."[36]

Both Matthews and Hemingway encouraged Gellhorn to write what she saw and what she knew of Madrid and send it to her friend at *Collier's*. Gellhorn later recalled the situation in *The Face of War*:

> A journalist friend observed that I ought to write; it was the only way I could serve the *Causa*, as the Spaniards solemnly and we lovingly called the war in the Spanish Republic. After all, I was a writer, was I not? But how could I write about war, what did I know, and for whom would I write? What made a story, to begin with? Didn't something gigantic and conclusive have to happen before one could write an article? My journalist friend suggested that I write about Madrid. Why would that interest anyone, I asked. It was daily life. He pointed out that it was not every body's daily life.[37]

She wrote about life in Madrid. It was her first article as a foreign/war correspondent and it was accepted by *Collier's* and after a second article Gellhorn's name was added to the masthead. One of the longest most fruitful and easy relationships in Gellhorn's life began in Madrid with *Collier's*. It was her professional home for eight years and would see her from her beginnings as a war correspondent in Madrid to her full maturity and the end of World War II.[38]

Gellhorn and Hemingway lived and loved through an exciting drama, but whereas Hemingway found and wrote about the war as "exhilarating sport," Gellhorn portrayed horrific suffering, courageous sacrifice, and an intangible sense of calm as she walked among the people of besieged Madrid.[39] "How can I explain that you feel safe at this war," she wrote to her *Collier's* readers, "knowing that the people around you are good people?" it is the beginning of Gellhorn's voice, a voice which will become extremely familiar to *Collier's* readers.[40]

Back at home, Eleanor Roosevelt struggled with the President over the need to change America's neutrality legislation.[41] Her hectoring him on this issue drew upon Gellhorn's letters from Spain, which seethed with indignation over America's unwillingness to assist a lawfully elected democratic government fighting for its life against a military takeover.

Their dialog on the issue of guns for Spain made for an important exchange. The war correspondent gave the First Lady information; indeed as Blanche Wiesen Cook puts it "ER's understanding about events in Spain came firsthand from Martha Gellhorn."[42] In return, Gellhorn received some naïve hope and belief she was effecting a change in American foreign policy, assuring Mrs. R from Spain that "the fight is far from lost here, but material is sorely needed."[43]

As far as Gellhorn saw it FDR's New Deal had revitalized US government's commitment to protecting and empowering the American people; now she believed his administration could and should defend democracy in the world at large. To Gellhorn the Depression at home and the Civil War in Spain produced uncannily similar scenes of human stamina in terrible times. She wrote to Mrs. Roosevelt that she saw "A curious similarity between the endurance I saw in the unemployed—a kind of heroism in peacetime disaster" and the suffering of Franco's victims in Spain.[44]

What she did not see and did not understand was that Roosevelt was continuing a hard fight at home to maintain funding of the New Deal. Gellhorn knew first hand the situation in America, but did not fully comprehend the complexity of the presidency and the domestic ramifications of Roosevelt asking an isolationist country while still in the midst of the Depression to support Spain and a civil war that most Americans had only a vague notion about. Gellhorn was writing for two very distinct and opposite audiences, the White House and the masses. She aimed at educating and calling both to action. This was very heady stuff for a 28 year old. Gellhorn was doing what her father had instructed. She was writing. While she continued to play upon her looks, her words on the page had substance and influence.[45]

Gellhorn's commitment to the *causa* of the Spanish Republic sent her back to Spain repeatedly between 1937 and 1938, inevitably worrying the First Lady to distraction. In one letter "Mrs. R" tried to persuade her young friend to come back to the White House and once more find it "rather a good place to work."[46] ER's close friend Lorena Hickok more or less rolled her eyes at Gellhorn's earnest exploits, describing her as "the glorious little fool."[47] Mrs. Roosevelt took Martha far more seriously and to heart, not only forwarding points of information to the President, but also welcoming Gellhorn, Hemingway and Dutch filmmaker Joris Ivens to the White House in July 1937 for a screening of the documentary *The Spanish Earth.* The staunchly pro-Republican film was directed by Ivens, written, narrated and partially funded by Hemingway. Though the two men had created the film, it was Gellhorn's connections that got it a private audience with the Roosevelts at the White House.[48]

In Spain, Hemingway was very dedicated to the cause of the Spanish Republic. Arguably, he was never an impartial journalist or war correspondent per se. He did however write far more prolifically about Spain both as war correspondent and as novelist. *For Whom the Bell Tolls* was his masterpiece. Reading it today, it is often strained in portions the use of "thous" and "thees" interferes with the modern reader more familiar with Spanish than its original audience and less tolerant of the awkwardness of phrasing. Hemingway wrote 31 dispatches from Spain and of those 28 were published. That is in addition to the script for Ivan's film, The *Spanish Earth* and the play *The Fifth Column.* Considering the length of time he spent in Spain, this was a solid output of journalism.[49] In comparison, Gellhorn was what she was, a novice, and an apprentice.

In Spain, Hemingway's articles were tinged with military strategy. War intrigued Hemingway and he enjoyed informing and educating others about the nuances of war. The role of military expert was one of his favorites. He will fall in to this mode, deeper and deeper and more acutely during his reportage during World War II. His later work would be overwhelmed by his desire to include military tactics and his personal prowess in understanding them. By the time of his World War II articles, he becomes the major player in his "journalism." However, Spain was before this acute turn.

Hemingway crafted his reports around the experiences of individuals. Highlighting the individual experience showed the reader the randomness and ruthlessness and indiscriminate nature of war, the human side of war. This is familiar because Gellhorn uses the same devices and templates. As she progresses as war correspondent and journalist she will continue to refine her style artistically.[50] For Gellhorn is it is a complete and utter departure from the self-centered narcissism of *What Mad Pursuit*. Martha Gellhorn is still telling the story, she is still very present, but this time, the eyewitness, not the lead actor.

The skill of focusing on an individual or episode is the common link between Hemingway and Gellhorn's work from Spain. Unlike the scenario suggested by Leicester Hemingway, that they edited and rewrote each other's work collaborating, then just putting one or the other name on the article, it is more likely that a certain synergy developed between the two. Hemingway definitely brought out the best in Gellhorn and she in him. William Branch Watson notes that the "conciseness and rhythm of his (Hemingway's) writing were really poetry disguised as prose."[51] This applies to Hemingway in

Spain, but could be applied even more so to Gellhorn's matured style.

Neither Gellhorn nor Hemingway got too deeply involved in the to the internal politics in Spain in their articles. That would have created confusion for readers, but both were unashamed supporters of the Republic. Both held a certain sense of outrage over the non-intervention policy, and both kept their accounts very simple and straightforward. They were writing what they saw from their perspective.[52]

Gellhorn took her apprenticeship from Spain and continued to hone her story telling skills. She maintained the story elements she developed in Spain, crafting stories around individuals, and bringing readers closer to human side of the action, without making the writing about herself.

Gellhorn's articles on Spain ranged from focusing on the effects of war on women and children in Madrid to life on the front lines. She spent time with the American International Brigade volunteers and paid eloquent in *Men Without Medals*:

> The Harvard student and the New York poet, lying on a dusty Spanish road in the July sun, not knowing what the end of it would be. They came a long way, all these men, to do what they believed they should do...In this war there are no rewards you could name. There are no Congressional Medals, no Distinguished Service Crosses, no bonuses for soldiers' families, no newspaper glory...The men who came all this distance, neither for glory nor money and perhaps to die, knew why they came and what they thought about living and dying, both. But it is nothing you can ask them about or talk about. It belongs to them. But you can think of it at night, with the window open, listening to the thud of trench mortars, the echoed hammering of the machine guns, the metal

ping of rifles, on the nearest front....You can think of it in the country, listening to the small noises at night. You can think of it with respect.[53]

Spain was Gellhorn's baptism by fire. She confronted her topic, "war," as she had done with the Depression, by immersing herself in every aspect. She prided herself on doing research and getting as much background knowledge as possible. She ardently believed that truth was a required ingredient in all of her work.[54] Her coverage of the Spanish Civil War fell into the pattern of the coverage of the Spanish American War in that one of her purposes was to raise awareness and support for the *causa* through her writing. Her time spent in Spain was an experience that educated her in the nuances of war and its effect on both the soldier and the civilian. Seven years earlier Gellhorn left America and set out for Europe to become a foreign correspondent. Martha Gellhorn left Spain a full-fledged foreign correspondent, moreover a war correspondent.[55]

Gellhorn returned to the United States safely in May 1937, to lecture for several weeks and promote the film, *The Spanish Earth*. Motivated to raise the consciousness of the American people and help them understand the significance of the war in Spain, she carried an urgent message.[56] As she later summarized it in *The Face of War* (1959):

> They were fighting for us all, against the combined force of European fascism...I felt...the Western Democracies had two commanding obligations: they must save their honor by assisting a young attacked fellow democracy, and they must save their skin, by fighting Hitler and Mussolini, at once in Spain, instead of waiting until later, when the cost in human suffering would be unimaginably greater.[57]

To her dying day, Martha Gellhorn viewed the Spanish Civil War as an anti-fascist war and the dress rehearsal for the coming war in Europe. For writers like Gellhorn and Hemingway and soldiers like Milton Wolff, the belief was that if Fascism could have been beaten in Spain, the war in Europe could have been avoided.[58] As Paul Holsinger notes the overwhelming feeling was that "in fighting fascism in Spain, the American volunteers…fired the first shots for the defeat of Adolf Hitler and his ilk."[59] This sentiment was relayed often to Eleanor Roosevelt and also to President Roosevelt as evidenced by memos in Mrs. Roosevelt's collection stating "The President has read."[60]

At the Second Writer's Congress (June 1937) Gellhorn addressed the subject of what writers could do about Fascism:

> We have the obligation of seeing and understanding what happens, of telling the truth, of fighting constantly for a clarification of the issues....A writer must be a man of action now. Action takes time, and time is what we need most. But a man who has given a year of his life, without heroics or boastfulness, to the war in Spain, or who, in the same way, has given a year of his life to steel strikes, or to the unemployed, or to the problems of race prejudice, has not lost or wasted time. He is a man who has known where he belonged. If you should survive such action, what you have to say about it is the truth, is necessary and real, and will last.[61]

It was her belief that writers had a responsibility and an obligation to do whatever was in their power to help raise the consciousness of the people in the world and to enlist support for causes of right. The motif from her youth was clear. Gellhorn was an ardent idealist, diligently trying to inform America about what she believed was a great menace, the Nazis and Fascists in Europe. In her own way she was a writer of action and knew where she belonged, on the front line journalistic fight against fascism. In her writing she attempted to show what she saw as real, necessary to understand, and at this point still believed journalism could make a difference.[62]

Later on in her life, she compared her efforts to dropping a pebble in a pond making small waves. In the end, she believed her responsibility was the effort to show the world the wrong taking place, and believed they would right them.[63] In addition to her writing, Gellhorn notes in a letter to Mrs. Roosevelt in February of 1938 she stated:

> I have made some 22 lectures in less than a month on Spain. I am not a lecturer and don't know how to do it, reasonably saving myself and not getting excited. I see these rows on rows of faces, often women and sometimes men, and think: I have on hour to tell them everything I have painfully learned and to shout at them if they go on sleeping they are lost.[64]

Gellhorn is mixed about her situation as writer of action in that she greatly disliked lecturing and celebrity, feeling that "if one is a writer, one should be a writer."[65] At the same time, she is repeating the example of her mother who spent a tremendous amount of time crossing the country raising awareness for the League of Women's Voters and raising money for Bryn Mawr.

After their common adventures on the fronts in Spain, Gellhorn and Hemingway's relationship was firmly cemented. They were a couple. When Gellhorn was not on assignment, she was with Hemingway in Sun Valley or Cuba.

[1] Hugh Thomas, *The Spanish Civil War*, 3rd ed. (New York: Harper & Row, 1986), 16.

[2] Ibid., 13-16.

[3] Martha Gellhorn, "Correspondence with Eleanor Roosevelt," ed. Eleanor Roosevelt (Hyde Park, New York: Franklin D. Roosevelt Library). AER Box #1424, FDRL, 5 January 1937.

[4] Herbert L. Matthews, *The Education of a Correspondent* (Harcourt, Brace and Company, 1946); Milton Wolff, August 20-26, 1999. Matthews and Gellhorn were friends. Milton Woolf stated he always felt that "Herb had a crush on Marty the whole time he was in Spain, but Hemingway was in the way."

[5] Gellhorn, *The Face of War* (1988), 52.

[6] Ibid.

[7] Jack Hemingway, Interviewed by Angelia Dorman , Sun Valley, ID, 15 August 1992. Hereafter cited as Hemingway Interview.

[8] Ibid.

[9] AER Box #1424, FDRL, 5 January 1937

[10] Gellhorn and Moorehead, *The Collected Letters of Martha Gellhorn*, 46.

[11] Gellhorn, "Notations on *A Critical Biography of Martha Gellhorn* by Jacqueline Elizabeth Orsagh," 61.

[12] AER Box #1424, FDRL, 5 January 1937.

[13] "Speaking of Pictures," *Life Magazine*, January 15, 1948, 8,9,11. The remnants of her "peace book" are in the closed until 2023 in the Gellhorn Collection at Boston University Archives.

[14] Letter to Pauline EH Collection January 14, 1937

[15] Merriman, who was the same age as Gellhorn, had been a professor of economics at the University of California was commander of the Abraham Lincoln Battalion until he was killed in the Battle of Teruel in January 1938. His replacement was 23 year old, Milton Wolff.

[16] For further discussion of the relationship between Hemingway and Gellhorn and *For Whom the Bell Tolls*, see Carl P. Eby, *Hemingway's Fetishism: Psychoanalysis and the Mirror of Manhood* (SUNY series in psychoanalysis and culture, Albany: State University of New York Press, 1999).

[17] Orsagh, *A Critical Biography of Martha Gellhorn*, 68.

[18] Milton Wolff, August 20-26, 1999.

[19] Phillip Knightley, *The First Casualty: The War Correspondent as Hero and Myth-Maker from the Crimea to Iraq* (Johns Hopkins University Press, 2004), 209.

[20] Gellhorn and Moorehead, *The Collected Letters of Martha Gellhorn*, 426.

[21] Gellhorn, *The Face of War (1959)*, 13.

[22] Ibid., 10.

[23] Ibid.

[24] Rollyson, *Nothing Ever Happens to the Brave*, 96.

[25] Gellhorn, "Notations on *A Critical Biography of Martha Gellhorn* by Jacqueline Elizabeth Orsagh," 84.

[26] Ibid., 64.

[27] Ibid., 86.

[28] Ibid.

[29] Virginia Spencer Cowles, *Looking For Trouble* (New York: Harper & Brothers, 1941), 3.

[30] Ibid., 8-11.

[31] Gellhorn Interview, 21 June 1995.

[32] Milton Wolff, August 20-26, 1999.

[33] Ibid.

[34] Orsagh, *A Critical Biography of Martha Gellhorn*, 85.

[35] Gellhorn, "Notations on *A Critical Biography of Martha Gellhorn* by Jacqueline Elizabeth Orsagh," 85.

[36] Ibid., 128.

[37] Gellhorn, *The Face of War (1988)*, 16. The author of that letter of introduction was Kyle Crichton of *Collier's*.

[38] Ibid.

[39] Peter Wyden, *The Passionate War: The Narrative History of the Spanish Civil War, 1936-1939* (New York: Simon and Schuster, 1983), 330.

[40] Gellhorn, *The Face of War (1988)*, 25.

[41] Blanche Weissen Cook, *Eleanor Roosevelt* (New York: Viking, 1992), 443-44.

[42] Ibid., 452.

[43] Martha Gellhorn to Eleanor Roosevelt, 24 April 1938, AER Box 1459, FDRL.

[44] Ibid., 23 May 1938.

[45] Moorehead, *Gellhorn: A Twentieth-Century Life*, 89.

[46] Eleanor Roosevelt to Martha Gellhorn, May 1938, AER Box 1459, FDRL.

[47] Weissen Cook, *Eleanor Roosevelt*, 496.

[48] Orsagh, *A Critical Biography of Martha Gellhorn*, 80-81.

[49] William Branch Watson, "The Hemingway Review," *Spanish Civil War Issue*, VII, No. 2, Spring 1988.

[50] Her edits of the pieces she chooses to republish in *The Face of War* and *The View From the Ground* also show editorial refinement. While Gellhorn stated she republished the articles more or less as they were printed in Collier's, there are cases where she omits fragments of

sentences, or entire paragraphs and inserts a short paragraph to improve the power and voice of the article. This is particularly true in her reprint of *Dachau*. Kate McLoughlin looks closely at the changes Gellhorn chose to make in Dachau in *Martha Gellhorn: The War Writer in the Field and in the Text*.

[51] Watson, "The Hemingway Review," 4.

[52] Milton Wolff, August 20-26, 1999.

[53] Martha Gellhorn, "Men Without Medals," *Collier's* 15 January 1938, 49.

[54] Martha Gellhorn, "On Apocryphsm," *The Paris Review*, Spring 1981, 295.

[55] Gellhorn, *The Face of War*, 16.

[56] Kert, *The Hemingway Women*, 253.

[57] Gellhorn, *The Face of War*, 7.

[58] Milton Wolff, August 20-26, 1999.

[59] M. Paul Holsinger, *War and American Popular Culture: A Historical Encyclopedia* (Greenwood Press, 1999), 223.

[60] AER Box 1459, FDRL.

[61] Martha Gellhorn, "Writers Fighting in Spain" *The Writer in a Changing World* editor Henry Hart (New York: *Equinox*, 1937), 67.

[62] The League of American Writers was a group of writers and artists affiliated with the Communist Party USA (CPUSA). The key to being included was not necessarily to be a member of the CPUSA, but to reflect the party line. Not being a member of the CPUSA and her direct access to the Roosevelts was considered a plus. It is hard to say if connection to the Roosevelts or her close connection to Hemingway got her included in the proceedings or if she was invited because of her published articles in *Collier's*. Whichever is the case, Gellhorn's speech was included in the proceedings and gives the modern reader a glimpse into her feelings regarding writers and war. It also cements her status as a liberal idealist activist writer.

[63] Gellhorn, *The Face of War*, 1.

[64] AER Box 1424, February 1938, FDRL.

[65] Ibid.

CHAPTER 6

MARTHA GELLHORN
FOREIGN CORRESPONDENT

Martha Gellhorn left Spain an accredited foreign correspondent with a professional home at *Collier's* magazine. *Collier's* next assignments for Gellhorn were the only non-war reporting she did during her association with the magazine. She reported on war preparations and the mood of the people in France and England, and the situation in Czechoslovakia. To her this series of articles was aimed at explaining to her readers the impending threat of war from Germany. Two reports during this period are from Czechoslovakia, the naively optimistic piece, "Come Ahead Adolf," published in August of 1938 and the other in December, "Obituary of a Democracy" after the German take-over. The fog of optimism in "Come Ahead Adolf" is layered loudly with Gellhorn's liberal reformer idealism.[1]

In the face of Nazi and Fascist intervention in Spain, Gellhorn's belief that Czechoslovakia would stand strong and hold fast face to face with the Wehrmacht was wishful thinking on her part. At this point in her life, she still did not understand that even with access to the Roosevelts, providing them direct information and impassioned pleas, there was little that would or could change the course of fate.

"Come Ahead, Adolf!" reads as if it was written by a cheerleader, Gellhorn described herself as one of a "Federation of Cassandras," who could see no possibility of defeat, even when it stared her in the face in the shape of the Heinlein's and the evidence of non-intervention in Spain.[2] The article does show a great deal of how Gellhorn thought. She still held on to her idealized childhood version of the accomplishments of the muckrakers and the power of the press; she was firm in those beliefs and carried them through to her journalism. Her philosophical baseline which she did not hide and stated most directly in *The Face of War* makes that abundantly clear:

> If people were told the truth, if dishonor and injustice were clearly show to them, they would at once demand the saving action, punishment of wrong-doers, and care of the innocent…I think I must have imagined public opinion as a solid force, something like a tornado, always ready to blow on the side of the angels.[3]

"Come Ahead Adolf!" began with Gellhorn's passion driving home the nature and age of Czech democracy, including details like a reference to a town's clock constructed in 1490 and the idea that the clock and Czech democracy had been around longer than America, coupled with the naïve belief it would continue to remain so even in the face of the current crisis. Whether Gellhorn believed her own article or hoped her praise of the strengths of the Czech resistance would influence German intelligence was hard to say.

She brashly quoted a Czech song of the day for the title, "Come Ahead, Adolf!" and proceeded to create a portrait of a country prepared to defend its democracy and freedom in the face of impending fascism. The plow shed to sword imagery was clear and was placed in the middle of the second column at a very eye catching level by *Collier's* editors. Gellhorn wrote about the haystacks that were not haystacks but "camouflaged pillboxes with machine guns and antitank guns" amongst the soldiers that "stand as quiet as scarecrows among the working peasants." In the next village, there were the Heinlein's and Nazi Swastikas in the windows.

Gellhorn continued her survey of the countryside adding her own military analysis regarding the Czech forces and the closeness of Dresden to Prague "a half hour flight for a bomber."[4] The American reader of 1938 might not have considered this fact as important as Gellhorn did, but she had seen what German bombers did in Spain and was correct in her observation. A half hour was close, especially close for bombers loaded and ready to attack, regardless of the pillboxes, soldiers in the country side and civilians with gas masks in the theaters. Of course, in a few years, the tables turned and Dresden was on the receiving end of one of the most massive bombing campaigns in history.

Orsagh noted that "infected with an optimism which hindsight can now brand as naïve, Gellhorn appraised the spirit and ability of resisting people," and promoted the idea that good will triumph over evil in spite of the fact that the Sudetenland was predominately Germanic and to a large extent pro-Nazi.[5] Gellhorn resented Orsagh's description and maintained that she was only "reporting on how the Czech's felt" as if one article could accomplish that task.[6] "Come Ahead Adolf" is Gellhorn at her youthful, idealistic, best, full of hope, full of the belief of right and good triumphing over evil. She did not entirely comprehend the lengths to which the European governments would go to avoid war, but she had a good natural grasp of Hitler's agenda and the lengths he would go.

In direct comparison to Gellhorn's first Czechoslovakia article, Margaret Bourke-White's photographs were featured in an article on Czech preparations published in *Life Magazine* on May 30, 1938. Bourke-White's article was published two full months earlier than

Gellhorn's. The essay showed the Czech war preparations, the weak border defenses "concrete blocks with which the Czechs would check Nazi tanks."[7] There was a direct parallel in the articles between Gellhorn's clock tower. Bourke-White showed the readers a clock tower, Gellhorn told the readers about a clock tower and used it to educate and make a point to the reader as to how civilized the Czechs were and for such an extended period of time, over 400 years and hence worthy of our sympathies. The articles also paralleled each other in their focus on the military aspects of potential German encroachment. It was at this point in the comparison that Gellhorn's article began to diverge

Life Magazine published numerous photographs of Czech peasantry, showing both the native Czech peasants, as well as the Sudetenland Germans. Bourke-White's photos were accompanied by a far more detailed examination of the 3.5 million Sudetenland Germans.[8] She also more accurately demonstrated the power and support of the Nazi factions in Czechoslovakia, with one page showing approximately 40,000 Czechs in a town square in a Nazi salute.[9]

Life's analysis of the Sudetenland German minority concluded most were "antimilitarist and Catholic" insinuating Hitler would have a difficult time gaining support from the group, an error Gellhorn also made.[10] *Life* promoted parallel ideas emphasizing that while saying "Heil Hitler" was considered treason in Czechoslovakia, the Czechs allowed the gathering of 40,000 Heinlists, thus demonstrating Czech democracy and tolerance in action. The photograph of the 40,000 Nazis was the most powerful symbol of the impending German occupation in either article.

While the word count was much shorter, the photos provided a far better background regarding the situation and *Life* even included a short bibliography at the end of the article. For the purposes of this discussion, the *Life* article proved that while Czechoslovakia was not a vacation destination, it was easily accessible to correspondents and photographers, both male and female. Gellhorn was accompanied by her friend Virginia Cowles on her first visit to Czechoslovakia. It also further demonstrated that Gellhorn was not the first or only woman journalist to cover the situation, nor the first or only published.

Gellhorn's subsequent visit to Czechoslovakia after the signing of the Munich Pact in September of 1938 led to her article "Obituary of a Democracy." During this trip, Gellhorn visited French General Eugene Faucher in an attempt to do something to influence and somehow help the Czech situation.[11] It was there and at that time she encountered diplomat George Kennan in Prague. Whether it was her own self-importance, her naïveté or her outside hope that she could make a difference, she waltzed in to the American legation and was indignant that nothing was being done for the Czechs refugees fleeing the Nazis. She demanded something be done. Kennan's perspective was from outside of Gellhorn's circle and at the time he wrote her off as "an ill-informed do-gooder."[12]

Gellhorn's experiences in Czechoslovakia were used as the background for her next novel, *A Stricken Field.* Jacqueline Orsagh noted that in the novel "Martha Gellhorn introduces Americans to the history of Europe in human terms."[13] A passage from the *A Stricken Field* accurately reflected where Gellhorn was professionally at this point in her career, "when we were younger...we covered three bell alarms and the morgue, but now we are successful and cover large international disasters."[14] Gellhorn's fictional counter part the young American reporter "Mary Douglas" gave the reader insight in to her assessment of the situation in Czechoslovakia and Gellhorn's interaction with the French military advisor to Czechoslovakia, Eugene Faucher who was the basis for the character "General Labonne" in *A Stricken Field*.[15]

Also from Czechoslovakia, she wrote an eight page report "Anti-Nazi Refugees in Czechoslovakia" sent directly to Mrs. Roosevelt. Gellhorn's report read much like her dispatches to Harry Hopkins, very straight forward, full of page after page of factual information and observation. It is not until page 5 of the letter that Gellhorn began to shape the information in a dramatic sense:

> There is not one of them who has not some trade and good work, habits, they have none of them in any way violated their position as guest of the Czechoslovak Republic, while in exile, (sic) Their demand is very simple: they would like to live.[16]

From that point on in her letter, she used many of the same devices she used in her journalism to create a report that was meant to bend the ear and touch the heart of the reader. Her reader was Mrs. Roosevelt and more often than not, also, President Roosevelt.[17]

Very much an echo of her *Collier's* style, Gellhorn's final page and paragraph are as follows:

> This story has no place probably in a report, but I shall add it nevertheless. I went to a refugee home in Prague; it was poor and crowded, with mattresses piled against the wall and people sitting about as they do, tragically waiting for nothing. At a table there were about fourteen young men and women, they were looking at a map of the world which they had taken from a geography book. They were looking to see where they could go, what country remained where a man could keep his freedom of conscience and live. They were silent. They knew that the great democracies were not opening their frontiers to them, they knew they were welcome no place, thought they had committed no crime

against society. So they sat and stood around the table looking at the map.

Then on of them put a finger on a tiny colored patch, Nicaragua. "Have you ever heard anything about Nicaragua?" he asked. No one answered but there was a vague murmur of "No." He said, "Maybe we could go to Nicaragua; maybe we could work there and live and be safe, maybe Nicaragua is a democracy.[18]

In the sense that writing style eventually takes over the writer, the journalist voice and Gellhorn's voice sounded more and more the same.

In the "Afterword" of *A Stricken Field* written in 1985, Gellhorn used the opportunity to fill the reader in on more of her biography. She added small snippets of information, dates from notes on hotel stationary, and created a narrative for the reader of her first trip to Czechoslovakia that not only repeated her anti-fascist motif, but also gave the modern reader the perception that her early work in Czechoslovakia was more focused and her opinions more mature than they actually were. The narrative afterword of A Stricken Field redeemed her *Collier's* articles, giving the reader the impression they were as well written as the "Afterword" itself. In ten pages, Gellhorn created the impression of a far more accomplished and complex "Martha Gellhorn, Foreign Correspondent, 1938."[19]

After her first trip to cover military preparedness in Czechoslovakia. Gellhorn and Virginia Cowles toured through the North of England, talking to people in the countryside and in the pubs. Gellhorn's article, "The Lord Will Provide for England," came from this trip. The article was terse and Gellhorn provided the reader with her sense of frustration with the English, and that was summed up by her sarcastic title. It was possible that Gellhorn was able to project some of her frustration with America's non-intervention policies by grilling the English about their attitudes.

The title of the article is a cynical play on the phrase. Gellhorn was impatient and appalled at British sentiments. She felt they should be outraged or at least aware of the serious threat of Nazi Germany. Gellhorn notes that "The Lord Will Provide for England" shows that I found the mental climate in England intolerable; sodden imagination, no distress for others beyond the scepter'd isle."[20]

Gellhorn began the article, "When you go do London, you forget about war." At the time of the Czech crisis the formal outbreak of World War II was still a year away.[21] Few Brits were overly concerned with the impending war, their faith in their politicians and a desire to enjoy the improved economy over shadowed their war thoughts. At the same time, few Americans were thinking about war in September of 1938, most Americans were concerned with extricating themselves from the Great Depression. But, Charles Colebaugh's editorial foresight stood and the article ran. Gellhorn began the article on England:

> If you buttonholed every passer-by in Piccadilly Circus and asked: "Do you think there's going to be a war in Europe?" ninety out of every hundred would say, "No," first, and if they stopped to think about it, they'd probably say: "Well, not this year anyhow..."[22]

The comments are probably not much different from what one would have found had they buttonholed every passerby in Time Square, but Gellhorn was not thinking that broadly. Gellhorn's mind was dominated by the war in Spain and the looming war in Europe. She had a difficult time emotionally reconciling the war she knew was coming, and the attitudes she saw in England:

It's all kept quiet, and you forget that across that choppy and uncomfortable Channel lies Europe, and you just think: I am in England, a fine green island, and everybody outside is a foreigner and very likely nasty, and here we'll tend to our own affairs, which means: Business as Usual.[23]

Clearly, however, much of her venom was directed at the English ruling class. She wrote HG Wells after leaving England:

Gellhorn is renouncing England…I detest your ruling class, really thoroughly and seriously. I despise them as mercenary and without any desires except those concerned with holding on to what they've got…and the worst of it is that the People put up with them, tip their hats, grin all over their faces and are delighted to be ruled, gypped, snubbed and lied to providing the gent who does it is a gentleman.[24]

Gellhorn wrote another article covering war preparations in France, and made a return visit to Czechoslovakia after the annexation of the Sudetenland. The articles were published in October and December of 1938, respectively. Her coverage of "large international disasters" continued even after a break in mid-1939 to complete *A Stricken Field* and accompany Hemingway to Sun Valley, Idaho. Hemingway, who was still married, met with Gellhorn in Sun Valley for a shooting holiday. He was completing work on *For Whom the Bell Tolls* and she was making progress with her work on *A Stricken Field,* in spite of the regular hunting trips and nightly dinner parties. Regardless of her later testaments to the contrary, they seemed to have a great time together. While Gellhorn was not particularly interested in hunting, she enjoyed the pheasant excursions and fishing trips with Hemingway. Hemingway and

Gellhorn spent a great deal of time with Gary Cooper and his wife Rocky, shooting during the day and dancing, dining and drinking at night. The period was well recorded by photographer Lloyd Arnold and his wife Tillie remembered the period of time Martha spent in Sun Valley as enjoyable for all concerned, both Gellhorn and Hemingway.[25] Later, Robert Capa captured their Sun Valley lifestyle for the pages of *Life magazine*. By all accounts other than Gellhorn's, it was a good time.

Collier's wanted Gellhorn to go to Russia via Scandinavia; even though Gellhorn was not very enthusiastic about the trip she took the assignment.[26] *Collier's* could not possibly have predicted the timing which Gellhorn would arrive in Finland. She arrived in Helsinki on the evening of November 29, 1939 and war promptly broke out the next morning at 9 a.m.[27] Gellhorn found herself in the middle of the Russo-Finnish war by accident and claimed to be the "only accredited female war correspondent" there.[28] She was also the rare foreign correspondent with a letter of safe passage from the President of the United States.[29]

She never made it to Russia, but toured the Finnish fronts and turned out five articles on the war for *Collier's*. Virginia Cowles arrived a few weeks later. Both American women, covered a war that is more or less forgotten, overshadowed by the outbreak of World War II. Cowles wrote about Gellhorn in Finland in her memoir *Looking for Trouble*.[30] Gellhorn also included a fictionalized version of her trip to Finland in her 1941 collection of short stories *The Heart of Another*.[31]

---

[1] Martha Gellhorn, "Obituary of a Democracy," *Collier's* 10 December 1938; Martha Gellhorn, "Come Ahead, Adolf!" *Collier's* 6 August 1938.

[2] Gellhorn, *The Face of War* (1959), 2.

[3] Ibid., 1.

[4] Gellhorn, "Come Ahead, Adolf!" 13.

[5] Orsagh, *A Critical Biography of Martha Gellhorn,* 93.

[6] Gellhorn, "Notations on *A Critical Biography of Martha Gellhorn* by Jacqueline Elizabeth Orsagh," 93.

[7] Margaret Bourke-White, "Czechoslovakia," *Life Magazine,* 30 May 1938. 54; Photo by Margaret Bourke-White, 52

[8] The estimates were 3.5 million Germans out of a total population of 15million, a little more than $1/5^{th}$ of the population.

[9] Bourke-White, "Czechoslovakia."

[10] *Life Magazine,* "Czechoslovakia," 55a.

[11] Richard Francis Crane, "A French Conscience in Prague: Louis Eugene Faucher and the Abandonment of Czechoslovakia," (Boulder Colorado: Columbia University Press, 1996).

[12] Nichols Thompson, *The Hawk and the Dove: Paul Nitze, George Kennan, and the History of the Cold War* (New York: Henry Holt and Company, 2009), 35.

[13] Orsagh, *A Critical Biography of Martha Gellhorn,* 147.

[14] Martha Gellhorn, *A Stricken Field* (London: Virago Press, 1986), 7.

[15] Crane, "A French Conscience in Prague: Louis Eugene Faucher and the Abandonment of Czechoslovakia." Crane published the fullest account to date of Eugene Faucher in Czechoslovakia. Gellhorn consulted with him on the project.

[16] AER Box 1424, FDR Library.

[17] Ibid.

[18] Ibid.

[19] Martha Gellhorn, *A Stricken Field*, 303-13.

[20] Gellhorn, *The View from the Ground*, 73.

[21] Ibid., 33.

[22] Ibid.

[23] Ibid., 34.

[24] Gellhorn and Moorehead, *The Collected Letters of Martha Gellhorn*, 66-67.

[25] Angelia Dorman, "Telephone Interview with Tillie Arnold," (22 August 1992).

[26] Orsagh, *A Critical Biography of Martha Gellhorn*, 106-07, 11. On September 11, 1939, President Franklin Roosevelt wrote a letter intended to assist Gellhorn in case she ran into any problems during her travels. The letter reads:

> To All American Foreign Service Officers;
>
> The bearer of this note, Miss Martha Gellhorn, is an old friend of Mrs. Roosevelt's and mine. For a period of five months or so, Miss Gellhorn will visit Russia and various other countries. Her purpose is to secure material for publication by one of our weekly magazines.
>
> I will appreciate it if you will kindly give her every assistance.
>
> Very sincerely yours,
>
> [Signed] Franklin D. Roosevelt

[27] Gellhorn, *A Stricken Field*, 311. In the Afterword of the book Gellhorn expounds on this period of her journalistic career.

[28] Virginia Cowles, *Looking for Trouble* (London,: H. Hamilton, 1941), 321.

[29] Orsagh, *A Critical Biography of Martha Gellhorn*, 110-11.

[30] Gellhorn approved of Cowles' *Looking for Trouble*. She got along well with Cowles from their first meeting in Spain and they were friends until Cowles' death. She felt *Looking for Trouble* was the best account of her life in Spain. She and Cowles wrote a play after the war, *Love Goes to Press*. In the play, Gellhorn wrote the dialogue for the Cowles character and Cowles wrote the dialogue and action for the Gellhorn character. It is a revealing portrait of Gellhorn as her friend saw her, funny, vulnerable and warm. Martha Gellhorn , Interview ,14 June 1995.

[31] Martha Gellhorn, *The Heart of Another* (New York: Scribner's, 1941)

CHAPTER 7

GELLHORN AND HEMINGWAY
WRITERS AT WAR

Gellhorn's relationship with Ernest Hemingway was complicated at best. Their affair began in Spain and the backdrop of the civil war, and continued through the end of the 1930s. Even before their wedding, she had incurred if not his wrath, at least his sulking, by leaving for Finland in late 1939 to cover the Winter War. As in Spain and Czechoslovakia, she continued to focus on the human cost of international conflict.

Hemingway, whose previous coverage of war had often seemed to treat it like a quintessentially masculine sporting event, stuck to sporting events pure and simple. He spent his time hunting in Sun Valley, in his soon-to-be wife's absence. When she returned, Hemingway showed his hurt feeling, and imitated his future expectations by having her sign a mock wedding contract and act of contrition:

> I the undersigned Mrs. Martha, or Mrs. fathouse pig...hereby guarantee and promise never to brutalize my present and future husband in any way whatsoever...I recognize that a very fine and sensitive writer cannot be left alone two months and sixteen days... [1]

And the last clause made it clear that continued globe-trotting would clearly be out of the question:

I am deeply sorry therefore and shall attempt...to make up to him for the wretchedness he has gone through and shall also attempt to protect him against the same wretchedness in the future.[2]

Hemingway more and more possessive of Gellhorn, and was upset and depressed by her departure from Sun Valley. Tillie Arnold recalled he moped about as "Poor abandoned Papa!" for several weeks, in contrast to Martha's excitement and sense of urgency to get back to the excitement of world events.[3] On one hand, Hemingway was lonely and needy. On the other hand, he was pleased and proud of Martha. He had taught her the ropes of surviving in a war, he had tutored her on her reportage and in many ways she was his protégé. Although, Gellhorn would be incensed by this characterization, she did learn her battlefield basics from Hemingway and Herbert Matthews, and like it or not, her writing was greatly influenced by Hemingway and her articles resonated with his influence.

After leaving Finland, she made a farewell stop in Paris during the Christmas of 1939. Later in 1959, she wrote "I said goodbye, with love and I bolted from Europe...I didn't think it would be a battle; I thought there would be a massacre, and I could not bear to witness another."[4] War hung like an ominous cloud over Europe and Gellhorn fled to Cuba where she spent the majority of her time working on fiction and listening to radio reports about the situation in Europe. She completed her book on Czechoslovakia, *A Stricken Field*. It carried the dedication "for Ernest Hemingway," just as Hemingway dedicated *For Whom The Bell Tolls* to Gellhorn. Both books went to press in 1940, the year of Gellhorn and Hemingway's marriage.

Gellhorn's initial aversion to being in Europe when the war broke out led her to China. She noted that "Journalism now turned into an escape route."[5] Hemingway accompanied her on this trip, as a working honeymoon.[6] No matter how much she wanted to mentally escape the reality of what was happening to Europe, she could not anticipate the difficulties of the journey to China. In the end she was also glad to have Hemingway with her to help deal with the hardships she encountered along the way across the Far East.

In an exchange between Hemingway and a reporter in an interview in San Francisco before they headed to the Orient, Hemingway was asked his opinion on how long the war would last. His answer was "In three months or 20 years." Gellhorn corrected Hemingway and inserted her opinion into the equation positing "five years."[7] Indicative of the state of their relationship at the time, Hemingway conceded to Gellhorn's assessment and amended his timeline to meet hers.[8] They departed San Francisco on February 1, 1941 on the *Matsonia* and after a tumultuous, storm tossed trip across the Pacific they arrived in Hawaii. The first leg of their trip from San Francisco to Honolulu foreshadowed the hardships of the rest of the journey.[9] This was not going to be in any way a romantic pleasure trip. In fact, the tempest tossed nature of the early journey also foreshadowed the relationship with Hemingway. Things started out in a conciliatory give and take manner and quickly disintegrated into disarray under the pressure of the hardships encountered in China.

In Honolulu, they were met by feature writer Elizabeth McDonald (McIntosh) and interviewed. The final column published in *The Honolulu Star Bulletin* is the typical coverage of celebrities arriving on the island. But, as McDonald recalled, Hemingway seemed tired, but was very charming. Gellhorn on the other hand did not seem to be worried about being pleasant or nice; she gave the impression of a very cold, brash, self centered and self-important personage.[10] This very much reinforces the Carlos Baker version of Gellhorn as cold, calculating and self-centered. This also helps reaffirm the idea that Gellhorn often saved her charm for those she felt deserved it.[11] However, it is clear in final paragraphs of McDonald's article, Gellhorn has already begun to narrow and shaped her journalistic biography:

> His wife [Hemingway's], whom he met in Spain first started her journalism career on the *New Republic*, later went to Paris to live and became (a) foreign correspondent for *Colliers*... She writes mostly descriptive pieces which are revised by the magazine editors to fit the news of the places she writes.[12]

The article concluded with brag by Hemingway regarding Gellhorn's ability to shoot, "She is an expert rifle shot, a protégé of her husband." And a testament to Gellhorn's love of fitness and the water: "She plans to do a lot of surfing and swimming during her island visit."[13]

Key in this brief news article were thematic issues that early Gellhorn biographers, like Carlos Baker bit off on and propagated, such as her protégé status and her short handing and streamlining her credentials. As noted earlier, Gellhorn's association with the *New Republic* was minor and benign. Also, as noted earlier, the implication that she went to Paris and became a foreign correspondent is more her wishful thinking than reality, but it is obvious the beginning of the mythology of Gellhorn is finding it way into print. All of which, she would revise, refine and redefine in her later biographical writing.[14]

China was a massive obstacle to manage. In 1940, there were very limited options for transportation in the vast country. Poverty was the common denominator across China, from travel and transportation to accommodations; conditions were substandard to say the least. Nothing in her previous travels compared to the difficulties on this journey.

The couple arrived in Hong Kong on February 22, 1941.[15] At that point, Gellhorn's juvenile romantic ideal of China was smashed. Hong Kong was filthy. Night soil (excrement) was carried out of the streets daily, and spitting was common place and disgusted Gellhorn. The trips to the fronts with Hemingway were far more difficult than any trip than she had ever made before or would ever undertake again. The best account of this journey is in *Travels With Myself and Another.* It was written almost 35 years after the trip to China and over a decade after the death of Hemingway. It can be viewed as Gellhorn's attempt to take some control over her role in what she terms as Hemingway "mythomania." While she did not portray herself in heroic terms, like Lillian Hellman in her memoirs, she did come across as funny, humble and slightly fragile, yet resilient heroine.

In *Travels With Myself and Another,* Gellhorn framed her journey into and out of China with her account of the flight in as an introduction and the flight out to mark the conclusion to her account.[16] The one and a half hour flight from Hong Kong over the mountains into China was turbulent. Departing around 4:30 a.m. from Hong Kong, the DC-3 made a steep spiraling climb to get to altitude of 14, 000 feet to begin their journey to Chung King. In an account written over 30 years later, Gellhorn uses her well honed ability to choose the minimum amount of words to convey the feeling of the situation and to deliver the maximum impact:

> We climbed, as if climbing a spiral staircase, in tight jolting circles over Hongkong (sic) until we reached fourteen

thousand feet. All lights went off except the dim light in the
pilot's cabin and we crossed the Japanese lines, brightly lit
far below. In half an hour, the storm hit us. I had been
watching the flickering exhaust flame on a wing, but the
wing vanished into cloud that looked grainy and hard as
granite. Hail sounded like a threshing machine. Everything
froze including the airspeed indicator.[17]

Using another technique Gellhorn perfected, she focused on the
pilot, Roy, and used his competence to reflect her panic at the
conditions:

Roy explained that if the speed dropped below 63 miles per
hour the plane stalled and went into a spin, but there was no
cause for anxiety; he opened his window a crack and judged
air speed that way; he'd done it often. The wind-screen was
a sheet of frost. Inside this cloud mass, elevator draughts
lifted and dropped the plane, one's stomach making the same
vertical movements. I had untroubled confidence in Roy, so
the behavior of the plane didn't disturb me but I was
perishing of cold. Behind the cabin, the passengers vomited
or hid beneath their blankets from the sound and the fury.
This lasted for an hour and a half, after which Roy remarked
the rest of the trip would be easy. We were still flying blind
in cloud but I thought it would be bad mannered to mention
that.[18]

The China National Aviation Company (CNAC) planes bounced
through the sky on their flights over the mountains crossing Japanese
lines on a regular basis. Gellhorn's trip that day had her landing on a
mud airstrip in Namyung, then taking off again and making a circuit
which led back to Hong Kong. Though, treacherous, the CNAC
flights were the easy part of the journey.

Covering the China-Burma road, the main difficulties Gellhorn
encountered were those of China itself, its vast territory, its war torn

countryside, the language and the primitive facilities. She had access to the fronts, translators and military officials, but facilities were limited. On their arrival, Gellhorn and Hemingway began a journey to the Canton Front roughly heading back in the direction of Hong Kong. What took an hour and a half by turbulent flight took nearly four harrowing days by land. There was an overwhelming amount of mud on the journey, poor billeting arrangements and it was as Gellhorn stated many times a "horror journey."[19]

Transportation was poor and difficult, large portions of the trip were spent on mule back, in a leaky over packed Chriscraft boat, the only one on the river, and in dilapidated motor cars.[20] The lack of health care led to a prevalence of disease, and the climate itself promoted insect infestations and various forms of jungle rot, which she contracted on her hands by the end of the trip.[21] Gellhorn travelled with cans of flit to use to keep the bedbugs and other biting insects at bay. Most of the hotel mattresses were unbearably insect-infested, despite Gellhorn's cache of insecticides. The board beds at the front were a luxury.[22] China was a consistent challenged to Gellhorn's obsession with hygiene.

While she was an experienced journalist and war correspondent by this point in her life, nothing in her St. Louis background or even Hemingway's wilderness jaunts in Idaho had prepared her for the hardships of this particular trip. The frustration of this journey was humorously summed up in a later in *Travels With Myself and Another* with description of a trip to an elevated out-house. After reaching the top of the "ladder, nervous about the bamboo structure but comforted by the mat screens" an air-raid began.[23] The villagers scattered and Hemingway, who had suggested she use the local duck pond to relieve herself, stood below laughing at her situation. Frustrated because she had decided to attempt to use some sanitary convenience, after days of inconvenience in the field, she elected to stay in the out-house, where she had "an excellent view" of the air raid. During the rest of the trip, Hemingway ribbed her, "what an inglorious death it would have been. M. intrepid war correspondent, knocked off in the line of duty. But where? But how, the press of the world inquires."[24]

In retrospect, in her account it was Hemingway's humor that diffused the sheer trauma of the whole trip. Both Hemingway and Gellhorn come across positively in her account. In many ways, her generous portrayal of Hemingway in the memoir allows the reader to see some of the better points of Hemingway's personality and many of the reasons he was such an attractive character. Keeping in mind this account of the trip was written decades after the fact, Gellhorn's humor under duress helps add grace and wit to her own construct of her persona of foreign correspondent.

After touring the fronts, Gellhorn was granted an audience with Chiang Kai-shek and Madame Chiang. The article that followed made Madame Chiang's day a lot like Eleanor Roosevelt's, only longer. It is, as Gellhorn admitted, "self-censored" due to the fact that they received hospitality from the Chiang's.[25] It is the only time that Gellhorn admits to this type of self-censorship in her work, and one of the few times in her career in which she is restrained in her political commentary. She was Edna Gellhorn's daughter and despite rejecting St. Louis life, she never rejected the manners and sense of society she received there. Of the Chiangs she wrote:

> They struck me as the two most determined people I had met in my life. Their will to power was a thing like stone; it was a solid separate object which you felt in the room. They were also immensely intelligent, gracious and, I thought, inhuman. But I had accepted their hospitality, and since they owned China, it would be as if I had visited them as a guest

and thanked them by writing unpleasant revelations about their house. I have never again accepted hampering hospitality.[26]

She balanced her meeting with the Chiangs with a clandestine interview with Chou En-lai. The interview with Chou En-lai never showed up in the pages of *Collier's* due to the American Government's official support of the Chiangs, but Gellhorn eventually wrote of the meeting years later in 1978.[27] What showed up in the pages of *Collier's* was reporting which was sympathetic to the Nationalist Chinese and an attempt by Gellhorn to help her readers understand the situation in China.[28] But, as with her other articles between Spain and Pearl Harbor, her articles were skewed to raise sympathy for the war against fascism from her readers.

When the journey was completed in China, Hemingway left for the United States, while Gellhorn stayed on an additional week in the Orient to tour other areas that she thought would possibly be affected by Japanese encroachment, Batavia, Singapore and Borneo.[29] Almost to provide a bookend to her journey *The San Francisco Chronicle* published a brief article on her arrival back in San Francisco. It is a fluff piece which focuses primarily on Gellhorn's appearance. She often joked and played down her appearance, but obviously it was important to her.[30] The reporter noted:

> Martha Gellhorn, reporter-wife of Novelist Ernest Hemingway can cope nicely with bombs, shells and machine gun bullets. But she can't handle the little outfits turned out by Batavia's better couturiers. She arrived in one of those outfits yesterday aboard the Chinese Clipper and was so depressed by her appearance she spent hours...indulging in the purely feminine past time – shopping.[31]

The latter part of the article gives Gellhorn's assessment of the possibility of war in the Orient. The reporter noted that "it is Miss Gellhorn's personal opinion that war between the United States and Japan is very remote."[32] Before the end of the year, the Japanese bombed Pearl Harbor and the US was at war with the Axis powers in both Europe and Asia.

Gellhorn's journey and reportage from the Orient failed on many levels. While she came clean about the self censorship in her reports on China in *The Face of War* and revised her stance, Gellhorn did not revisit her flawed Pacific war predictions, nor did she deal with the shortcomings of her article "Singapore Scenario" published in August 1941.[33] Throughout her career, Gellhorn was a better journalist than prognosticator of geopolitics. She also found it far easier to point out and correct errors in others, than in herself.

"Singapore Scenario" compares Singapore to a movie set, and Gellhorn noted that "all that really needed is Miss Marlene Dietrich in the role of waterfront siren, vamping the army, navy and air force."[34] The framing of the article in terms of a Hollywood movie of the era makes the piece come across as shallow and flippant. It is a portrait of the settled Europeans, young soldiers and gay young women and the British complaining about the lack of discipline of the Australians. However, she ended the article with a cascade of the positive questioning:

> How well the Japanese can stand up to well armed opposition. How terrific the Australians and Indian troops, schooled in years of border warfare, can be in battle. How good Singapore's air force will be, once the uniforms get dirty and the dinner parties cease and the business in hand is to bring down enemy planes.[35]

The article has the same resonance as many of Gellhorn's other articles, but lacks a grasp of the situation. Gellhorn never revisited her assessments of Singapore as she did with her articles on China. Within months of the Singapore article, the Europeans who survived the first onslaught of the Japanese would be interned. Regardless of Gellhorn's nonchalant tone, the men, women and children, soldiers and civilians were to experience hardships at the lash of the Japanese comparable in severity to those interned in Nazi camps in Europe.[36]

All in all, during the first half of 1941, Gellhorn, reported for *Collier's* on the Canton Front, the China-Burma Road, the defenses of Singapore, Hong Kong and the Dutch East Indies. Her experience in Asia cured her of any childhood nostalgia about the Orient. Gellhorn found it over crowded, impoverished, filthy and in 1959 laid out her suggestions:

> A good six-point program for China during the next hundred years would be: clean drinking water—at least at stated places; sewage disposal everywhere; a government-issued birth control pill; and an agricultural scheme which would guarantee the bare minimum of rice required to prevent the death by starvation of any Chinese. With these matters attended to, they could begin on a universal health service, attacking cholera, typhoid, typhus, leprosy, amoebic dysentery, malaria (malignant and benign), and all the other ills the flesh is heir to, but more heir to in China than in any other country I know. After that, it would be time to build schools and fill them. And then, finally, but how far in the future, the moment might have come to say a word about democracy.[37]

Gellhorn's observations and suggestions are interesting in the fact that they reflect her thinking and philosophy. Again, as when she was working for the New Deal, birth control tops the list after clean water and sewer. Her list progresses to its final critical point of schools to educate the masses before a working democracy could take root. This is very similar to and reflects the need for the type efforts Gellhorn's grandmother's made to educate the mass influx of immigrants and in-migrants that flooded St. Louis at the end of the 19th century and her parents desire to promote and support education. In addition, she sees a need to implement programs which would mesh with her father and grandfather's interest and work in sanitary conditions and public health. Her childhood illusions were replaced by the values she grew up with.

After returning from the Orient, Gellhorn was not on an active war front for a year and a half. A large part of the reason she did not return to a front more immediately was because Hemingway wanted to her to stay with him, safe and at home in Cuba. Gellhorn was not idle during the period. She initially used the time to recuperate from exhaustion due to the trip to the Orient. Then, she finished a volume of short stories, *The Heart of Another.* During this period Gellhorn produced one of her most important pieces of fiction, *Liana.*[38] *Liana* was born out of a short investigative trip Gellhorn took for *Collier's* in the Caribbean, traveling throughout the area on a potato boat reporting on military preparedness.[39]

Gellhorn's journey through the Caribbean is chronicled in two *Collier's* articles and her later memoir of "horror journeys" *Travels With Myself and Another.* The trip served as inspiration and research for her next work of fiction, *Liana.* The novel was about beautiful black woman trapped on a Caribbean island. While certainly not autobiographical, since Gellhorn was not an illiterate black woman trapped between cultures and contemplating suicide, the novel *Liana*, written between late 1942 and early 1943, demonstrated her belief that even life in a tropical paradise could be hell for a woman experiencing a stifling marriage, deferred dreams and any hopes of change fading.[40] In the afterword of *Liana*, she noted:

> *Liana* grew from a wonderful lunatic journey through the Caribbean in 1942, about which I have written elsewhere. My transport was a potato boat, a thirty-foot sloop with one sail and a hold for hauling potatoes between the islands. We were becalmed on a very small island for four days. I lived in a swoon of joy, hoping the wind would stay dead. I thought that chance had brought me to the last best place in a crazed suffering world. These little islands were always isolated, but at that time—the hurricane season and German submarines—totally isolated. I realized that Eden is a subjective state, and even here people could manage to make themselves unhappy.[41]

With *Liana* , Gellhorn finally demonstrates her ability think and write outside the confines of her own life. The book is poignant and warm, and the protagonist is not a thinly veiled version of Martha Gellhorn. It is also in no way a story lifted directly from her personal life. Ironically, the last book she wrote as Mrs. Hemingway was her best selling novel. She noted that it did not top the Best Sellers List, it made "the respectable middle."

Liana worked far better as a novel than did Gellhorn's journalistic reports from her Caribbean trip. She wrote an eleven thousand word account of the trip which amused her editor, but did not make the pages of *Collier's*.[42] What did make Collier's were two articles "Holland's Last Stand" and "A Little Worse Than Peace." Both articles contain comments that are paternalistic at best, and unwittingly racist at their worst. Like "Singapore Scenario," these articles are not Gellhorn's best reportage, but because of that they deserve further examination.

In her Puerto Rican article, "A Little Worse Than Peace," the immediate focus was on the economic impact of the war on the island. This is a theme she hits upon again in Surinam in "Holland's Last Stand." The first page of "A Little Worse Than Peace" focused on the change in shipping products coming in and out of the country. As she was in "The Lord Will Provide for England" and "Singapore Scenario," Gellhorn is eloquently patronizing regarding her assessment of the Puerto Ricans understanding of the war:

> To most people of Puerto Rico, this was is a strange and mysterious trouble, like a hurricane destroying far-off places you have never heard of. They do not know where the path of the wind is, or if it will ever blow this way. All they know is what they can feel themselves.[43]

She shifted focus to the stevedores and used them and their plight to lead the reader along. Later, she used the slum conditions observed in Puerto Rico as the lifestyle her heroine Liana marries to escape.

Gellhorn was supremely aware of the lack of cleanliness, describing living conditions:

> (the) hot smell of dirt –dirty bodies, dirty walls, stale refuse, open sewers. You walk down paths in which rain stands, and gathers garbage from the houses. All kinds of people live here…there is a woman cooking lunch in a tin can for her two small children and husband…in most of these houses there are not even the crudest facilities. [44]

The resonance of the article and the subjects she included are reminiscent of her reports to Harry Hopkins during the New Deal. Gellhorn was providing a broad assessment of living conditions, much as she did while working for the FERA. Unlike in "Singapore Scenario" and "The Lord will Provide for England," Gellhorn did not sink as deeply into the sarcasm she seemed to reserve for the British during this period.

Toward the end of the article, Gellhorn's tone shifted to paternalistic condescension in her description of the lure and attraction of the Army for Puerto Ricans. While one of the women she interviewed said that her desire to have her husband join the Army was "Por la patria," Gellhorn focuses only on the improvement in living conditions to be gained by young Puerto Ricans in the Army, especially those with families, due to their increased pay. Gellhorn admits that "It is amazing to think of a war as a health cure."[45] The comment serves to highlight the difference and social distance between Gellhorn and those whom she writes about.

The Puerto Rican article was long, running 5 pages in *Collier's.* Gellhorn's final page illuminated more of her prejudices. She notes

> The thin top layer of society has not been seriously affected by the war. If you have the money you can buy what you need…Daily life seems to go along, almost untroubled, and – with exceptions – the upper classes seems unaware of the war s previously they were indifferent to the conditions of peace…the upper class of Puerto Ricans has chosen to inhabit a self-centered world where the two main occupations are making profits and making politics.[46]

Gellhorn then took a stab at the "carryings on" of corrupt local politics, not unlike a muckraker. However, her audience was not particularly concerned with the machine politics of a small protectorate in the middle of the Caribbean. The article dragged long, it was over written, droll and unobtrusive. Even with her ability to frame an article and establish a cadence with the words, Gellhorn was hit or miss with her articles for *Collier's* from this period.

"Holland's Last Stand" fares slightly better, probably because it is a shorter article. The article appeared in December 1942 and in spite of the title, it is only war reporting in the barest sense. Later in *Travels With Myself and Another* Gellhorn draws on the unpublished portions of her trip and *Holland's Last Stand* to fill out her account of her journeys during this period.

Gellhorn started the article with another quick stab at her readers' general level of geographic competency:

> When the American soldiers write home saying that they are in Surinam, they get letters back saying that it must be very exciting in Australia or that it must be terribly hot in West Africa… It lies hot, unknown and unimportant between British and French Guiana on the northeast coast of South America…By air, Dakar is 1,500 miles away and Miami is 2,323 miles.[47]

It is difficult to tell if she is being supercilious, trying to educate the reader or is making a stylistic stab. Gellhorn quickly moved from her introductory geographic paragraph to Surinam's colonial background and current value to the United States. Overall the piece is flat and unexciting, possibly because the situation in Surinam was so far from the action of the war and a rather unexciting outpost.

One detail which is included in both the *Collier's* article and later in Travels *With Myself and Another* is her account of the toe chiggers. Gellhorn established with her accounts of her trip to China her entomophobia, and blends her running account of her fear of insects with the unbearable weather in the Surinam article:

> The jungle, called the bush, looks like a solid snarl of green ropes. There are no trees on the field and the heat rises around you in solid layers. You stand, a little sun-blinded

with the heat folded around you, and a dry wind picks up the sand and rattles against the white office building against the gas drums that grow all around the office. A man says "You better not walk in the sand with those shoes, you'll get chiggers under your toenails. Some sort of local chigger you have to cut out" [48]

During this period before and after the Caribbean trip, Gellhorn and Hemingway were living at the Finca Vigia in Cuba. Gellhorn's obsession with cleanliness unnerved Hemingway, who had did not have issues with bugs or dirt.[49]

Gellhorn used a full magazine page setting up the scenario in Surinam. This was far more introductory space than in her later articles. Also, in the article, Gellhorn again allowed the reader to see some of her own personal social prejudices:

> The village came out to see us and cluster round Bush Negros are small men with well-developed shoulder muscles (from paddling the native canoes and lumbering) and with spindly legs. The women are small, too, and after they are fifteen years of age, they are old and increasingly ugly... [50]

As she continued, her portrait of the natives equates their lack of awareness with their social and racial backwardness.

> I asked one serious looking savage what they though of the war.
> "War" he said very puzzled.
> "You know," I said "all the fighting that is going on."
> "No, no, no," he said; "we no fighting. We do nothing bads."
> "Not you," I said; "the war in Holland"
> There was grave though for a while. Then the type said, "We sorry for Missy Wilhelmina."
> "Why?"
> "She cannot go home."

> That was as far as I ever got on the subject of the war.
> Beyond the queen, whom they regard as a personal friend if
> not a near relative, the Bush Negros are as innocent about
> war and politics as they are about life, love and clothing.
> They are very nice, amiable people, if you like savages, and I
> am told you can get use to their smell.[51]

Gellhorn made an attempt at economic analysis of the situation, noting that, "Of course, here, as everywhere in the Caribbean American money has capsized all local economics."[52]   But, she does not follow through on the idea or what it meant to have capsized the economies or what it will take to correct the situation. Ironically, her older brother George was involved in American attempts to stabilize the post- World War II Latin American economies as a USAID employee.

What is clear in the final articles from Asia and the Caribbean was that Gellhorn had perfected a basic template, but not her focus. She started an article with a basic set up, then included herself and her experience and voice as active narrator, but often she could not get the right focal points for these. When she got the template and the focus right, her articles rose to a standard well above the average published pieces of the day and many were so outstanding that they have not been paralleled.   Gellhorn was about to be drawn to the biggest story of her life, the Second World War. When she returned to Europe and was on the war front, the pattern/template of her writing was already set and the intensity of the war front forced her to a laser like focus, and this left little room for extraneous material.

In the midst of reporting on World War II, she was forced to get to the telling of the story and to do that in a rapid, efficient manner. Martha Gellhorn's voice became loud and clear, and at the same time she used that voice as a "tape recorder with eyes" omitting as much of her unconscious class commentary and internal biases. When Gellhorn applied that laser focus to just tell the story, that was when her articles worked best. Comparing her final Asian articles and her Caribbean articles to her war reporting in Spain opens up the plausibility that Hemingway and Matthews did help with the editing of her first articles from Spain. Those articles are not at the level she achieved later in her European Theatre of Operations (ETO) World War II writing, but far exceeded her Asia/Caribbean articles.

It is difficult to discern what happens when any relationship ends. It is complicated because there is always his story, her story and the true story. The true story is difficult to find in the best of circumstances, but with two strong willed ego driven writers, it is far more complex. No one will ever know exactly what happened between Gellhorn and Hemingway. Gellhorn had over 35 years after his death to set the record straight and cement her side of the story and, more often than not, refused to do it. Her position was very Garboesque – she insisted she wanted to be left alone regarding that topic.

Gellhorn made a choice not to write a traditional autobiography. She had opportunities to correct the things she saw as errors in the numerous Hemingway biographies which were published during her lifetime. She clearly had the opportunity to have the last word, or at least a say as to her side of the situation, and chose not to. Gellhorn's pose refusing to write or comment on their relationship is not surprising. A part of the persona of "Martha Gellhorn" has to do with the fact she's the only one of his wives who divorced Hemingway. From a feminist point of view, she stood up to him, laid out her own legacy and in the face of his constant assault on her character, she took the high road. This is all part of the Gellhorn mystique. Gellhorn was quite proud of her humility when it came to dealing with her life with Hemingway.

When she did commit parts of their life together to paper in *Travels With Myself and Another*, she veiled Hemingway as UC (Unwilling Companion) writing a humorous likable portrait. In some ways, the use of "UC" Gellhorn is overtly refusing to capitalize on the Hemingway name. At the same time, the use of "UC" did not erase the reader's knowledge of who "UC" was and in many ways just served to bring more attention to Hemingway's presence.

What is clear is that the two had a good time together from the beginning of their relationship up to the period when Gellhorn and Hemingway stayed in Cuba for a year from November 1942 through late October 1943. It was during this extended period of togetherness that Gellhorn began to become restless and the seeds of the disintegration of their marriage were sown.

A window into the complexities of their relationship and its final collapse is provided by the letters that are available. A key in getting a glimpse of Hemingway's side of things is through his letters prior to their breakup. After their marriage was over, Hemingway's letters and comments about Gellhorn were venomous and brutal and he attacked her no holds barred in 1944 and ever after. But, on March 16, 1943, that was not the case. Hemingway wrote a 6 page letter to Gellhorn pleading his case as her dutiful and concerned husband:

> I have tried to help you in every way and when I was here I
> have tried to take every single thing of management etc off
> you hands and keep your time free for writing. I tip-toe in
> the mornings, I make the servants be quiet, I tell people who
> want to bother you they cannot see you, I ran the house and

so forth when you were gone quite a long time at Christmas holidays and tried to have everything neat and clean and good when you came back, and I have no greater joy than seeing your book develop so amazingly and beautifully.[53]

From the letter it was clear he felt Gellhorn was angry at him, noting:

> Now I come back to an atmosphere as though I were some sort of villain of the piece. Bong, I think you have me mixed up with some awful people you have been reading about or seeing in the movies or maybe the husband of the lovely mulatta.(sic)[54]

In rebuttal to Gellhorn's claim that she was trapped with Hemingway in the Caribbean, Hemingway wrote insightfully of her situation and her moodiness:

> You are as free as air. Nobody keeps you here. You have always gone away whenever you wanted to. There is no need to destroy me because you feel you have to go out into the world again...Nearly always, when you away hate me as the nearest and most articulate object because what you hate is not being as free and as young as we both were when we started for Europe.[55]

And in an echo of Gellhorn's father's letter to her regarding her first novel, her life with de Jouvenel and desire to be a writer, Hemingway said:

> Your beauty will go.
> Your youth will go.
> Everything will go except writing well and the only way to write well is to do it in spite of bloody what all and not to use your surroundings and the sensitiveness of your soul and the

bastard that I am as an excuse for why you can't write. So maybe why not try writing?[56]

The letter in its entirety provides the clearest glimpse of Hemingway's feelings regarding Gellhorn before everything completely soured. He was doting, supportive, caring. He gave her good advice, hard advice and criticism. He was her most constructive critic and her greatest advocate.

The letters they exchanged during the fall of 1943 and in to January of 1944 were civil and Gellhorn wrote him long letters full of her feelings and opinions. It quickly became clear that Gellhorn thirsted for adventure and the wider world, and was at home at the war. Hemingway, however, was satisfied staying in his Caribbean paradise, holding court in Havana and on his boat, the *Pilar*.[57]

The most important story of the century was unfolding and Hemingway had no problem with letting it happen without him. He felt as though he had been to enough wars and was not eager to join this one. It is possible he was losing his nerve. It is also possible that it became clear to him that luck cannot hold out forever. Hemingway was extremely superstitious and might not have wanted to try his luck. Gellhorn's patience had worn thin.

She could not convince Hemingway to accompany her, so she left for the European Theater of Operations (ETO) on her own in October, 1943. Gellhorn was restless and had had enough of the isolation in Cuba. She set out to cover the war in Europe, leaving Hemingway fuming. She had to get back to the world conflict, and tried to make her husband understand that the woman he loved could not do otherwise. Covering the air war over Britain and the slow advance in Italy, she continued to write urging Hemingway to get into the war.

After her departure in October 1943, she regularly wrote long loving letters to Hemingway. In a letter dated December 9, 1943, sent from the Dorchester Hotel in London. Gellhorn continued to plea for Hemingway to join her. She wrote:

> I love you, I miss you and I wish you were here where you would be the darling of all, and as you are so much smarter than me, I would not have to work so hard because you could do my thinking for me. I do wish you would come. I think it's so vital for you to see everything…I restrain myself from sending you cables saying my dearest Bug please come over at once, for fear you'd think I was sick or something and that would be a dirty trick on you. But that is what I would like to do.[58]

Gellhorn continued to try to coax him to Europe. She also insisted that if she failed to follow her calling she would stagnate both professionally and personally:

> But I believe in what I am doing too and fiercely regret having missed seeing and understanding so much of it in those years [the time spent Cuba with Hemingway] and I would be of no use to you in the end if I came back before I was through.[59]

Gellhorn apparently had some sense that her marriage to Hemingway might be falling apart, but still she felt she had to be honest about her inability to come right back to the safe and peaceful home they had made together in Cuba. "Please forgive me," she wrote in a pained letter, "[but] when I think of it [domestic life in Cuba] it is like being strangled by those beautiful tropical flowers that can swallow cows."[60]

In December of 1943, she made it absolutely clear that she had no intention of coming home any time soon. Being together in the Orient had done little to cement their personal relationship and their time in the Caribbean, even though Gellhorn was busy writing her one of her best pieces of fiction, was as she noted a "prison."[61]

But after a few weeks she gave up trying to persuade him and shifted her concentration to defending her insistence on following her convictions and career:

> It is a great big world and I love to walk about in it and look at it. I am very lucky as a woman to be able to do this because most women can walk nowhere and see nothing...[62]

It was both a statement of her refusal to be a stay-at-home woman, and a stab at other women as she saw them.

Hemingway was feeling sorry for himself and drinking heavily. He became more and more deeply depressed and upset by Martha's absences. The house was uncared for and a mess, Hemingway spent most of his time drinking at home, or on his boat drinking and on U-Boat patrols, an endeavor Martha saw as an excuse to obtain fuel during war time rationing.

By January 1944, Gellhorn gave up all together trying to persuade her husband to join her overseas. Having neglected to write him for some time, she offered a postmortem on her hopes that he might join the war after all: "I used to write you letters, urging you to come and then I stopped, realizing that I had no right to interfere, that I cannot possibly judge for you, that in fact you might not like it here."[63]

The gauntlet had been thrown down and Hemingway was infuriated. Whereas, he had only been mildly irritated before at his wayward wife, he now lashed out in grand form. After a brief trip home to Cuba in March 1944, Gellhorn finally prevailed upon him to come to Europe. She had returned to Cuba and the Finca to make one last stab at salvaging her marriage to Hemingway. Instead the relationship blew up in her face and after that point she was finished with Hemingway and the marriage. Somewhere between her head and her heart, she wrote Hemingway and their relationship off as unsalvageable. It is hard to say what could have salvaged things. Gellhorn inquired of a young interviewer regarding her marriage and sex life, noting "good sex was the glue that seemed to hold things together."[64] From her accounts, there was no glue to hold the relationship together. That does not mean that the end of the relationship was easy.

The visit in March 1944 marked the end of the relationship for Martha. Hemingway raged at her. His tone and feelings had come 180 degrees from his letter of one year earlier. The kindness in his heart had been replaced by his depressive mood and further washed away by his alcoholism. Gellhorn had begged and pleaded with him to go to war and Hemingway was going to go to war, to war with Gellhorn. He could have written for any magazine or newspaper in America, but he chose to pursue the one assignment that could hurt his wife the most. Hemingway offered his services to *Collier's* magazine.[65]

They booked separate passages for Europe. Hemingway flew to London. Gellhorn spent 17 days crossing the heavily mined Atlantic in a boat loaded with dynamite.[66] When they next met in London in May, their encounter proved brief and bitter. His presence in London did nothing to save the marriage. Hemingway had joined the war after all, but he did his best to make Miss Martha regret it. Although several more rounds were to be fought, Gellhorn was finished with Hemingway, and she would not let his presence stop her from covering the war. Gellhorn was no more deterred by Hemingway's than she would be when the Public Relations Officers

(PROs) denied her permission to cover the D-Day invasion from the front.[67]

Hemingway had a very difficult time reconciling the end of this marriage. This time he did not do the leaving, nor did he have an immediate replacement in the wings. However, in short time after his arrival in England, he met Mary Welsh, began an affair and had his replacement Mrs. Hemingway lined up.[68] Gellhorn attempted to try to at least be civil with Hemingway after his final arrival in Europe to cover the war. This, in spite of the fact that he signed on with *Collier's* magazine and bumped her from the top slot in the ETO, and several of his mixed drunken attempts which bounced between trying to woo her back and bully her back at the same time.

As for Gellhorn, she was going to cover the war. The biggest story in history was unfolding, everything in the past decade had prepared her for this moment, and nothing was going to stop her from covering it. Not Hemingway, not the PROs, not the fact she was a women, nothing was going to stop her from her appointment with providence.

It was a transformative period in history and in the personal and professional life of Martha Gellhorn. Hemingway and Gellhorn's relationship as war reporters during their years together was a tempest set against the stage of spreading global conflict. These two writers embraced and confronted the Second World War from Spain to China to France, even as they went to war with each other, and neither writer emerged unaffected by the struggle.

Gellhorn's skills as a novelist improved during her years with Hemingway, although she never equaled him as a novelist, then or later. However, her own talent as a frontline correspondent continued to dwarf his self-conscious and stilted attempts at reporting his own personal war. Hemingway's inability to look at

Gellhorn's gifts with anything other than a mixture of consuming jealousy and maudlin self-pity served as an early indication of the incipient decline of his own creative faculties. But, this is mostly clear in retrospect. What was most evident to all and sundry at the time was that Mr. and Mrs. Ernest Hemingway in the end truly became two writers at war, and neither of them emerged from the period unscathed.

---

[1] As quoted in Kert, *The Hemingway Women*, 338-39.

[2] Ibid.

[3] Dorman, Interview with Tillie Arnold, 22 August 1992.

[4] Gellhorn, *The Face of War* (1959), 69.

[5] Ibid.

[6] Gellhorn and Hemingway were married in Cheyenne, Wyoming en route from Sun Valley to New York on November 21, 1940. Orsagh, pp. 116-117, 119-120, and Kert pp. 411, 417, 422-423. Mrs. Roosevelt offered her assistance again. The previous letter taken to Finland was updated by President Roosevelt to include the "Far East" and her name was amended to Mrs. Martha Gellhorn Hemingway. On the china trip, they worked together as a team for the first and last time since Spain. Their marriage was short and stormy with marital strive peaking in late 1943 and early 1944, and the official divorce on December 21, 1945.

[7] "He Was a Right Guy and the Woman with Him Was Good Looking: For the Hemingways There'll be no Farewell to Arms," *San Francisco Chronicle*, 31 January 1940.

[8] Ibid.

[9] Jeffrey Meyers, *Hemingway: A Biography* (Da Capo Press, 1999), 357; "He Was a Right Guy and the Woman with Him Was Good Looking: For the Hemingways There'll be no Farewell to Arms."

[10] Interview Elizabeth (McDonald) McIntosh, Woodbridge Virginia, August 22-23, 2009. Elizabeth Peet McDonald worked for the Star Bulletin after her 1936 graduation from the University of Washington in journalism and Japanese. She was hired by Scripps Howard and was covered the bombing of Pearl Harbor, and was then transferred to cover Eleanor Roosevelt at the White House. She was recruited by the OSS and sent to the Far East, with tours in India and China. After the war, she wrote an account of her OSS experience "Undercover Girl." Was employed by the Voice of America and later went to work with the CIA, retiring in the 1972. During her retirement she wrote an account of the women in the OSS *Sisterhood of Spies* and is currently the editor of the OSS Society magazine. Mrs. McIntosh is currently 97 and lives in Woodbridge, VA

[11] Carlos Baker, *Ernest Hemingway: A Life Story* (New York,: Scribner, 1969). The first exhaustive biography of Hemingway, Gellhorn cooperated to a certain extent with Baker. In the biography, to a certain extent, Gellhorn comes across much as Hemingway saw her calculating, conniving and as someone who used him for her own means. In line with her attitude regarding most things written about her, she was never happy about how she came across in the book.

[12] McDonald (McIntosh). Elizabeth, "Hemingways Answer Call to Adventure," (*Honolulu Star Bulletin* 5 February 1941).

[13] Ibid.

[14] For later biographical writing refer to *The Face of War* (both 1959 and 1988 editions) *The View from the Ground* and *Travels with Myself and Another.*

[15] Peter Moreira, *Hemingway on the China Front: His WWII Spy Mission with Martha Gellhorn* (Washington, DC: Potomac Books, Inc., 2005), 210-11. While much of Moreira's thesis of Hemingway as spy is overstated, Moreira does provide an accurate concise timeline for Gellhorn and Hemingway's travels.

[16] Gellhorn frames her article "Dachau" beginning with awaiting an airplane ride out of Germany, focusing on Dachau, then ending the article again on board the plane.

[17] Martha Gellhorn, *Travels with Myself and Another* (New York: Putnam, 2001), 15-16.

[18] Ibid.

[19] Ibid.

[20] Gellhorn, *Travels with Myself and Another*, 22.

[21] There is a tendency to view travel in undeveloped parts of the world as inconvenient but rather safe. That is not necessarily true. Case in point is that of Marguerite Higgins who died in 1966 after contracting leishmaniasis covering the war in Vietnam. The potential for viral and fungal infection was there and could be fatal.

[22] Gellhorn, *Travels with Myself and Another*, 46.

[23] Ibid., 35.

[24] Ibid.

[25] Gellhorn, *The Face of War (1988)*, 75.

[26] Ibid., 70.

[27] Gellhorn, *Travels with Myself and Another*, 52.

[28] Martha Gellhorn, "These Our Mountains" *Collier's,* 28 June 1941.

[29] "Martha Gellhorn, Reporter - Wife of Ernest Hemingway, Clippers Into Town," *San Francisco Chronicle* 28 May 1941.

[30] Gellhorn, "Notations on *A Critical Biography of Martha Gellhorn* by Jacqueline Elizabeth Orsagh," 86. Gellhorn takes exception to her being described as having "smart looks and fine, well-fitting clothes" writing "no, no…I was poor not dressing at Saks." That she takes the time to comment on a brief complimentary comment about her looks speaks again to the fact that it was important for Gellhorn to control her persona.

---

[31] "Martha Gellhorn, Reporter - Wife of Ernest Hemingway, Clippers Into Town."

[32] Ibid.

[33] Martha Gellhorn, "Singapore Scenario," *Collier's,* 9 August 1941.

[34] Ibid., 20.

[35] Ibid., 44.

[36] For a more in-depth survey of the conditions of Europeans held captive by the Japanese, see Karl Hack and Kevin Blackburn, *Forgotten Captives in Japanese-Occupied Asia* (New York: Routledge, 2008).

[37] Gellhorn, *The Face of War* (1959*),* 70.

[38] Orsagh, *A Critical Biography of Martha Gellhorn,* 158-63. *Liana* is a major step for her development as a fiction writer. She for the first time removes the autobiographical aspect that had marked her fiction prior to this time, creating a three dimensional heroine, that in no way is a thinly veiled version of Martha Gellhorn. *Liana* deals with the conflict of a very innocent and naive woman reconciling herself to the fact that it is a "man's world" and the insignificance of her needs within that world. In the end the reconciliation is too difficult for Liana and she chooses a way out on her own terms, suicide. Orsagh notes that this "feminist book emerges from the period when her relationship with Hemingway suffered increasing hostility," she also adds that "Gellhorn may well have been reacting to years of sexist press and...'protective discrimination.'"

[39] Baker, *Ernest Hemingway: A Life Story,* 377.

[40] Martha Gellhorn, *Liana,* 1st Edition (New York: Scribner's Sons, 1944).

[41] Martha Gellhorn, *Liana* (London: Virago Press, 1987), 224.

[42] Gellhorn, *Travels with Myself and Another,* 89.

[43] Martha Gellhorn, "A Little Worse Than Peace," *Collier's,* 14 November 1942, 14.

[44] Ibid., 15.

[45] Ibid., 85.

[46] Ibid., 86.

[47] Martha Gellhorn, "Holland's Last Stand," *Collier's,* 26 December 1942, 25.

[48] Ibid.

[49] Moorehead, *Gellhorn: A Twentieth-Century Life*, 198.

[50] Gellhorn, "Holland's Last Stand," 28.

[51] Ibid.

[52] Ibid., 26.

[53] Princeton University, Firestone Library, Special Collections, Carlos Baker Collection (henceforth Baker) CO365. Letter, Gellhorn to Hemingway, 13 December 1943;

Baker Collection, Ernest Hemingway to Martha Gellhorn, March 16, 1943.

[54] Ibid. The "mulatta" he refers to is the main character in Gellhorn's book, *Liana.*

[55] Ibid, 2.

[56] Ibid, 6.

[57] T. A. Mort, *The Hemingway Patrols: Ernest Hemingway and His Hunt for U-Boats*, 1st Scribner hardcover ed. (New York: Scribner, 2009). Mort provides a detailed look at Hemingway's sub hunting period. Also see Abbreviated copy of Ernest Hemingway's FBI file, Community Library, Ketchum Idaho. He came up with a scheme to hunt German U-Boats with his fishing buddies and with Gellhorn's connections to the Roosevelts, the *Pilar* was outfitted for the job.

[58] Gellhorn and Moorehead, *The Collected Letters of Martha Gellhorn*, 156.

[59] Baker, Letter from Gellhorn to Hemingway, 13 December 1943.

[60] Baker.

[61] Ibid.

[62] Gellhorn and Moorehead, *The Collected Letters of Martha Gellhorn*, 159.

[63] Baker. Gellhorn letter to Hemingway, 5 January 1944.

[64] Martha Gellhorn, 21 June 1995.

[65] The rule was that each magazine was to have only one lead reporter in the ETO. Hemingway's choice of *Collier's* relegated her to second status and also allowed Hemingway to control portions of her expense accounts.

[66] Moorehead, *Gellhorn: A Twentieth-Century Life*, 215.

[67] Harold Acton, *Memoirs of an Aesthete, 1939-1969* (New York,: Viking Press, 1971), 258. Acton was a Paris censor and he singled out Gellhorn as having "the best written and most vivid" of the articles submitted to him.

[68] Moorehead, *Gellhorn: A Twentieth-Century Life*, 217.

CHAPTER 8

EUROPE 1944-1945
MARTHA GELLHORN'S WAR

Her pieces are always about people. The things that happen to her people really happen and you feel it as though it were you and you were there. ... She hates to get up in the morning...But when she is at the front or getting there (she has worked in Spain, Finland, China), she will get up earlier, travel longer and faster and go where no other woman can get and where few could stick it out if they did.

> Ernest Hemingway
>
> March 1944[1]

Hemingway gave that assessment to Amy Porter of *Collier's* for her *This Week* column despite the collapse of their marriage and the entailing personal upheaval. The work Gellhorn produced during the war from the fall of 1943-1945 in Europe is her most refined and controlled; the reportage contains not only the readable historical perspective of her earlier articles, but are also skillful pieces of craftsmanship. Martha Gellhorn's journalistic ability had developed to its full potential. Gellhorn's voice is clear, firm and focused. She had perfected her rhythm and cadence and her laser like ability to focus on the right individuals to place in her articles at just the right point in order to allow the reader to both empathize and connect to the bigger picture.

She made no claims of being a totally objective authority; her political and personal opinions are, as always, found woven throughout her work. The people in her articles were real, and flesh and blood. Gellhorn stood firmly by her work as a record of her own reactions to the human legacy of war, a witness. Gellhorn viewed objectivity as "both rubbish and boring."[2] That does not mean she viewed journalism as propaganda, far from it. She noted news agencies as "literally send[ing] out a bulletin, the time, the place etc." that is objectivity, but she continued:

> If you are seeing something happen, that you are so brain dead and stony hearted you have no reaction to it strikes me as absolute nonsense. And you see appalling things happening to people, well how could you not describe, you are describing what you see and what you see is awful.[3]

The articles of this period were very carefully written and designed, delivering their messages subtlety, effectively and with artistry. As a whole they presented us with one woman's personal history of the final period of World War II and the clearest glimpses of the Martha Gellhorn who broke rules, chased the story, saw the history of her time and wrote it.

By November 1943, she was eager to get back to the European front and follow the war where ever possible for the duration. Immediately after her arrival in London, Gellhorn connected with Virginia (Ginny) Cowles at the Dorchester Hotel in London; they had been together in Spain, Czechoslovakia, England, Finland, and now together again in the ETO. Cowles had been actively covering the war for *The Sunday Times* and *The Daily Telegraph*, while

Gellhorn was in the Orient and the Caribbean with Hemingway. Ginny was probably one of the most well connected correspondent's in London.[4] Cowles helped Gellhorn arrange for a place to base herself in London. After Gellhorn settled in, she headed to North Africa and poured herself into the situation at hand. She got back up to speed and back in the groove of being a war correspondent.

Everything had prepared her for this moment in time. In Spain, she learned the ins and outs of war, the direction of shells, the sounds of bullets, when it was time to duck, when it was time to run and when it was time to just stay still. Hemingway had been an excellent instructor in those points. As well, she had written enough pieces for *Collier's* to have a basic template for her articles, the compression of time and events narrowed her focus in on the most important details needed to fill and balance her template. The end of her apprenticeship, combined with her natural talent and the story of the century were all in the crosshairs, and Gellhorn produced some of the finest journalism of the 20th century.[5]

Gellhorn began writing articles almost immediately after her arrival in the ETO in 1943. However, they do not begin to show up in print until March 4, 1944. Then, her stories appeared in rapid succession, and a month does not pass without a story from the war by Gellhorn for 16 consecutive months. The ball began rolling in March of 1944 when *Collier's* published four of her pieces in succession over a four week period. Beginning with "Children are Soldiers, Too" published on March 4, 1944, followed by "Three Poles" on March 18, 1944, "Hatchet Day for the Dutch" and "English Sunday" March 25 and April 4 1944 respectively.

Of the first batch of articles published, "Three Poles" was the one with the most substance and gravity, and the one which prefigures her best form and the subject of her masterpiece article on "Dachau." "Three Poles" began with irony of the German's and their kindness toward animals, juxtaposed with the German's treatment of the Poles. There was an underlying indignation regarding the chaos and loss in war. The deportations of Poles, typhus epidemics and her reporting on the deaths of two and a half million Jews, all foreshadow her article on Dachau.[6] "Three Poles" was included in the 1988 edition of *The Face of War,* but was missing from the first 1959 edition.

While she did not include "Children Are Soldiers, Too" in *The Face of War*, it is important primarily because it was Gellhorn's first article on England since her scathing evaluation of the nation in "The Lord Will Provide for England" in 1938. This time Gellhorn found the England that she would come to love, the England the Germans could not bomb in to submission. In "Children are Soldiers, Too," she began praising the teenagers of London:

> They are fifteen and sixteen years old now, and they are at home in the war. They have never bought food except with ration books, or clothes except with coupons. They grew up to find trenches in the playgrounds, bunks in the subways, queues for everything, and they have never had a date except in the blackout….Almost before they began to notice where they lived, they saw their streets bombed; they take the curious gaps or the gutted houses of the neighborhood for granted.[7]

London would continue to be a gutted city, with the rehabilitation of the city taking decades and the majority of work was done by the generation of young Londoners in the article. Gellhorn's description captured the essence of their spirit:

> They are so at home in the war, since it is all they know, that they have to think twice before they can remember what

peace was like. These are the poor kids of London, the cockneys, speaking a rare and funny language of their own, which is sometimes as hard to understand as a foreign tongue. They are short and strong, not beautiful at all, but made of some material that endures.[8]

All in all, between March 1944 and June 1944, *Collier's* ran seven of Gellhorn's articles.

It was clear to everyone in the ETO, soldiers and civilian, that the invasion was going to take place very soon. Troops and materials were stockpiled in England and troops and ships were in motion. While the date was classified and only finalized just before the invasion, invasion was in the air.

In the pre-dawn hours of June 6, 1944, Hemingway no doubt savored a certain victory over Gellhorn as he joined the Allied armada steaming toward the Normandy beaches. He believed that Gellhorn, lacking his privileged frontline correspondent credentials, would have to hear about the D-Day invasion at a press briefing in London later that morning.[9]

As Hemingway subsequently recalled his exploits in the landing craft, he began what would over the next few months become a familiar pattern of exaggeration and egotism in his war reportage. Insisting that the sailors could not have found the beach without him, Hemingway neglected to mention in his article that he was then barred as a noncombatant from setting foot on the beach with the disembarking soldiers. Nonetheless, his readers were told that "we had taken the beach."[10] Actually, Hemingway was the one who was taken; even with his efforts to handicap her, Gellhorn beat him to Normandy.

Hemingway's reportage of Europe during this period can be summed with the same comments Philip Knightley made on his performance in Spain, nearly a decade earlier: "his performance was abysmally bad...his emphasis on his own close location to the action smacks of boastfulness; his accounts of blood, wounds and severed legs are typical of his desire to shock."[11]

Unlike Spain, however, this war was not a new lease on his life as a writer. *Across the River and Into the Trees* was not *For Whom the Bell Tolls*. Easily Hemingway's greatest gain from his foray into the ETO was not in his fiction, but in the tremendous addition of fodder to bolster the Hemingway myth. As well in *Time* magazine correspondent Mary Welsh, he found a woman correspondent available in the ETO who was willing to shift from a career as a writer to a career as Mrs. Ernest Hemingway. The whole experience was a Bimini boxing match wrote large and the prize was an egress into domesticity. Hemingway's decline had begun and for the remainder of his life a large portion of his time would be spent as the larger than life "Papa" Hemingway. While his proponents will point out that he followed his lifelong habit of writing almost every day, he only produced two exceptional works after the war, *The Old Man and the Sea* and *A Moveable Feast*. He also spent a great deal of his time after the war telling anyone who would listen how poorly he had been treated by Martha.

Assigned to a hospital group, Gellhorn was supposed to wait in England for reports and then follow the nurses onto the Continent, somewhere around D-Day+7. [12] However, she was not going to miss the story of the century and the solution to the situation just required ingenuity. She noted, "I felt like a veteran of the Crimean War by then ...I had been sent to Europe to do my job, which was not to report the rear areas or the woman's angle."[13]

Gellhorn had been under fire, suffered through hardship journeys and the inconveniences of covering war, but her major test in Europe would be getting through the red tape of the Public

Relations Officers (PROs). The fact she was a woman made it sometimes difficult to get to the front line. As for D-Day, she is the earliest documented woman correspondent on the beach.[14] Gellhorn made it to Normandy and beat Hemingway to the beach.

By her own account, Gellhorn snuck under several fences then locked herself in the lavatory of one of the first hospital ship that crossed the channel to pick up the wounded from the blood-soaked Normandy beaches. Stowaway Gellhorn let herself out of the hospital ship's toilet when the coast had cleared. Pitching in, she helped out wherever possible.

In *The Face of War* Gellhorn indicated that the Army Public Relations Officers (PROs) were difficult to deal with and that is most probably an overstatement on Gellhorn's part. It was a Navy PRO, Barry Bingham Sr. who arranged for Gellhorn to be attached to a group going ashore to pick up the wounded.[15] Bingham recalled in 1984, that Martha Gellhorn arrived on ship. In his office shrieking in tears, crying:

> that S.O.B. took everything from me and now he's taken the only good story I ever had. *Collier's* gave him (Hemingway) the beach assault and reassigned me to the woman's angle of a hospital ship."[16]

That ride to the beach arranged by Bingham got Gellhorn ashore earning the distinction of being one of the few journalists to make it to the beach during the active part of the Invasion, and the only woman to do so. After all she had been through with Hemingway, she had to get a certain amount of satisfaction from overcoming all the obstacles in her way and scooping Hemingway.

More importantly than who scooped whom, Gellhorn wrote the best articles published in *Collier's* about the invasion. She used the opportunity of being there and took in as much of what was going on as possible. From the experience, she produced two documentary important articles, "The First Hospital Ship" and "D-Plus One: The Prisoners." They are small pieces of the mosaic of the larger reality that was D-Day.[17] Joining the stretcher bearers in their chores, she could thus rightly claim to have hit the beach long before Hemingway's eventual arrival on French soil.[18] Gellhorn wrote about an experience characterized more by the desperate life-saving toil of others, than the false machismo of taking a beach. She found heroism to write about, heroism that was not about her, in glaring contrast to Hemingway's account. She found that heroism in the faces and the words of the wounded themselves on board ship:

> They were a magnificent enduring bunch of men. Men smiled who were in such pain that all they can really have wanted to do was turn their heads away and cry, and men made jokes when they needed their strength just to survive. And all of them looked at each other saying, 'Give that boy a drink of water,' or 'Miss, see that Ranger over there, he's in bad shape, could you go to him?'" [19]

Making her way to the beach head, Gellhorn waded ashore in the cold waist high water along with troops from the Hospital Ship. She wrote:

> This had been an ugly piece of beach from the beginning and they were still here, living in foxholes and supervising the unloading of supplies. They spoke of snipers in the hills a hundred yards or so behind the beach, and no one lighted a cigarette. They spoke of having not slept at all, but they seemed pleased by the discovery that you could go without sleep and food and still function all right. Everyone agreed the beach was a stinker and it would be a great pleasure to get the hell out of here sometime.[20]

The wounded on board had faced those same beaches less than 24 hours before when the situation was far more intense. Gellhorn describes an experience and the reactions of a typical wounded lieutenant. Young, pale and with a bad chest wound, he suddenly rose and looked out:

> His eyes were full of horror and he did not speak. He had been wounded on the first day, had lain out in a field and then crawled back to our lines, sniped at by the Germans. He realized now that a German, badly wounded also in the chest, shoulders and legs, lay in the bunk behind him. The gentle-faced boy said very softly, because it was hard to speak, "I'd kill him if I could move."[21]

The German at the brunt of this remark was, in fact, an Austrian conscript. He'd spent a year fighting in Russia, six months in France and had been home all of 6 days during the time. Wondering if he would ever get home again, he gently asked Gellhorn "whether wounded prisoners were exchanged." She assured him that he had nothing to fear. "The Austrian said, 'Yes, yes.'" Then added quoting him," So many wounded men, all wounded all want to get home. Why have we ever fought each other?"[22] Speculating that perhaps the tearful Austrian came from a gentler race, Gellhorn wrote, "He was the only wounded German prisoner on board who showed any normal human reaction to this disaster."[23] This was an enormous concession on Gellhorn's part, she had a great deal of anger pent up against the Germans and it had continued to built up since Spain. However, it is possible that some of her compassion for the Austrian was there because Gellhorn's father was from Breslau in Germany or of her Austrian/Czech Grandfather Fischel.[24]

As for the overall scenario on board ship, Gellhorn captured it in a nutshell:

> If anyone had come fresh to that ship in the night, someone unwounded, not attached to the ship, he would have been appalled. It began to look entirely Black-Hole-of-Calcutta, because it was airless and ill lit. Piles of bloody clothing had been cut off and dumped out of the way in corners; coffee cups and cigarette stubs littered the decks; Plasma bottles hung from cords, and all the fearful surgical apparatus for holding broken bones made shadows on the walls. There were wounded who groaned in their sleep or called out and there was the soft steady hum of conversation among the wounded who could not sleep. That is the way it would have looked to anyone seeing it fresh—a ship carrying a load of pain, with everyone waiting for daylight, everyone hoping for the anchor to be raised, everyone longing for England.[25]

She laid low for a short period, returning to Italy to distance herself from the London PROs and reported on the war "in the company of admirable foreigners who were not fussy about official travel orders and accreditation."[26] It is possible Gellhorn inflated her situation with the PROs. It is difficult to say.

Gellhorn is probably legitimate in the claim that the Army PROs were unhappy about her journey to Normandy. However, no record of any type of admonishment has been found.[27] Lee Miller on the other hand was in a forward area where she did not have clearance and took photographs of a "classified" event, the first use of napalm at St. Malo. Miller was stopped, locked up and detained for several days. After Miller was released and she flew under the radar continuing to cover the war and eventually the PROs forgot about the incident. Examining the SHAEF records, it is clear women were not encouraged to be out of their allowed areas. Those were the areas where service women were stationed and no further ahead. There is no verification that any harsh actions were taken against individual women who pushed that boundary, whether it was Lee Miller, Margaret Bourke-White or Martha Gellhorn or any other woman covering the war.

The more astute women avoided this problem by dodging the PROs whenever possible. Questions of a women's place at the front usually arose after the fact, as a story or photograph was being wired via the censor's home.[28] It is possible that since Gellhorn's articles were so positive and well written, the PRO office just let the dust settle on the situation.[29]

Gellhorn's writing was well-researched and the information was reliable and experience based. Her body of work from World War II presents the reader with numerous portraits of the individuals affected by the war. The articles she wrote during the 1944-1945 period are in the vanguard of war reporting; they are about people and the effects of war on people, from a variety of perspectives. She also wrote them in such rapid succession that it would have difficult for her to have attempted to create a motif in her work. When she poured herself into the war, the rapid succession of events and the need to work at a fierce pace meant her articles roared onto the page. The motif, the template, the rhythm of her language and ability to choose just the right details was the result of moment and her previous years of writing for *Collier's*. Everything in Gellhorn's life and career had led her to this particular moment and place in time.

Whether, she was writing of a young RAF pilot who has just spent three hours in the saline baths working to move his fingers a quarter of an inch.[30] She described the soldier:

> [With skin] burned so tight that he could scarcely move his
> mouth and the words came out in a shy mumble. The face

was absolutely expressionless, so set that it looked dead, but the shape of it was still intact. Two bright-blue eyes stared out of the scarred face and watched the stiff hands that bent ever so slightly under water. The rest of him was the fragile, tender body of a young boy, for after all nineteen is only a young boy.[31]

Or the young, tired Lieutenant in Bastogne in the midst of the mass confusion that was *The Battle of the Bulge*:

The survivors of the 101st Airborne Division, after being entirely surrounded, uninterruptedly shelled and bombed, after having fought off four times their strength in Germans, look—for some reason—cheerful and lively. A young lieutenant remarked, "The tactical position was always good." He was very surprised when we shouted with laughter. The front, north of Bastogne, was just up the road and the peril was far from past.[32]

On the pages of *Collier's,* these soldiers came alive with accuracy and respect, not glamour, pity or petty heroics. And, in contrast to Hemingway's articles from this period, her articles were not about herself.

Gellhorn's front-line coverage included time on the Italian front, the D-Day Invasion, the Battle of the Bulge, a mission in a P-61 *Black Widow* night fighter, as well as the occupation of Germany. There were difficulties for a woman getting to these fronts. They had to manage their own logistics and they maintained a certain level of concern regarding the PROs, but women still got to the front.

For a fictional account of this period, see Virginia Cowles and Martha Gellhorn's play, *Love Goes to Press.* Set on the Italian front, the Annabelle character based on Gellhorn works to romantically revive her relationship with another correspondent. It is clear that while one might want to read Hemingway as the love interest, he was not. For Gellhorn, that relationship was over. A switch had flipped, eliminating any and all possibility or desirability of a reconciliation with Hemingway.

The play however is a good glimpse of Martha Gellhorn. Cowles makes her (the Gellhorn character) warm, funny, and vibrant. It is a unique portrait of the day to day demeanor of Gellhorn through the eyes of her friend and for that alone the play is significant.[33] In the introduction to *Love Goes To Press*, Gellhorn mentions that while she was living at Sessa Aurunca, it was the only time during the war that she actually lived in a press camp. It was also only time she claimed to have had the correct travel orders which allowed her the luxury of living there and the ease of sending copy directly back to her editors at *Collier's*.[34]

Gellhorn produced several articles from the Italian fronts. Her first, "Visit Italy," was written prior to the D-Day invasion and her bump to second status at *Collier's*. The title refers to the tourist posters found all over Europe, prior to the war, and the irony it evoked in the circumstances of early 1944. Most notably for the purpose of understanding the war in terms of what it meant to be in the line of fire, "Visit Italy," was a harsh look at day to day life under constant fire.[35]

En-route to visit the French first-aid stations in San Elia, which Gellhorn described as a place "which used to be a town and is now a mass of blown up masonry."[36] Like so many towns and villages in Italy. The tactical situation faced by the Allies follows:

> The mountains of Italy are horrible; to attack always against heights held by well-entrenched enemy troops is surely the worst sort of war. Nothing can help the infantry much in mountains: Germans dug into the stone sides of these cliffs can survive the heaviest shelling. Tanks cannot operate. So

at last it is the courage and determination of a Frenchman against the courage and determination of a German. The French have been taking their objectives.[37]

The objectives came at the usual price of lives and limbs. At the aid station Gellhorn ran into two troops who had been injured when a shell exploded near the telephone line they were repairing. The Frenchman lost an eye and his friend from Martinique's leg was almost completely severed. Martha wrote that:

> The blind man made a tourniquet of telephone wire to stop his friend's hemorrhage, and then, because the torn leg was hanging by skin and tendons only, he cut the leg off with his clasp knife.[38]

The colonial soldier mourned his lost leg but he was alive, unlike the ambulance driver, a very pretty girl who had "been killed on the road to San Elia."[39]

Beyond her continued look at the losses and obstacles faced in Italy, in "The Gothic Line" and "The Carpathian Lancers" Gellhorn included details of Italy that might have fit well into a guidebook for the tourist of wars. According to Martha,

> This field grew huge dead cattle. They lay with their legs pointing up, and their open eyes were milky and enormous, and the air stank of their swollen bodies. ... Aside from the hideous dead animals everything looked lovely, with the Adriatic a flat turquoise blue and the sky a flat china blue and the neat green hilly country of the march ahead.[40]

Italy was still picturesque, minus the devastated towns, the pillboxes, the ever patient mine fields, the huge cemeteries, and the mass confusion and rot of war.

Needless to say, the soldiers needed some type of distraction to take their minds off of the war, if only for a moment. Something was needed on occasion to remind them that they too were human beings once and if they survive, they might be again. The question was, how do you fit in R&R in the middle of a war? The answer was: Anyway, anytime or any place you can, never mind the mine fields and artillery. Gellhorn was privy to a break in the fighting and one of those brief moments:

> Since the war had so delightfully stopped, and since it was beautiful weather, and since Second Squadron was in reserve near us and doing nothing in particular, we decided to go swimming. There was a slight snag because no one had had time to investigate the beach and the approaches to the beach for mines; but as the Poles said, if you spent your life always considering mines it would be quite impossible.
> We decided to walk side by side or closely following each other, on the grounds that it would not be fair for just one of us to explode. There were no mines, at least we did not step on any, and there was the warm pale sea and a beach of smooth white pebbles... We swam about, observing with interest our artillery was shelling the Germans to the right, and that the British engineers were probably detonating mines in Ancona to our left, since there were bangs and great black clouds rising from that port. Then we began to plan what to do in case the Germans broke through and we were in swimming during this operation. We decided it would be wisest to just go on swimming.[41]

It was R&R on the stunning Adriatic. By this point in the war, dying during a swim was probably preferable to stepping on a land mine on the way to the privy or dealing with the hangover of her personal life. What Gellhorn left out her articles and *The Face of War* were her trysts with soldiers in the middle of this incident and other intense moments. She viewed it as volunteer work to keep up the spirits of the soldiers.

Wary of the PROs, Gellhorn continued to maintain a low-profile and in *The Face of War* she wrote that "by stealth and chicanery" she made her way to Holland.[42] It was probable that the PROs had more or less forgotten about her. However, it was only during the Battle of the Bulge that she openly re-attaches herself to an American unit. From the Bulge on to Dachau, the 82nd Airborne Division becomes Gellhorn's unit and as the 82nd Airborne pushed forward, she wrote frantically article after article. Her finest articles were written under the protection and cover of the 82nd.[43] That came from the top; General James Gavin okayed Gellhorn's attachment to the Division. He also became Gellhorn's lover. Echoing her mother's remark, Gellhorn took up with the bravest of the brave soldiers, Gavin.

The peaceful Belgian country side was shattered as the last great German offensive of the war exploded in December, 1944.[44] The situation went from "fluid" to "contained" and back to "fluid;" all in all it was a bloody mess, as mass confusion permeated the surrounding region. Thunderbolts strafed overhead, cars, jeeps, shoes, helmets and bodies littered the roads.[45]

The situation stabilized on the first day of 1945 and Gellhorn brought the reader back to the heart of the matter and the heart of her work:

There were many dead and many wounded, but the survivors contained the fluid situation and slowly turned it into a retreat, and finally, as the communiqué said, the bulge was ironed out. This was not done fast or easily; and it was not done by those anonymous things, armies, divisions, regiments. It was done by men, one by one—your men.[46]

Soldiers were not the only ones who suffered during the war. In a war fought town to town, if your town was unfortunate enough to be in a strategic location, the war was fought on your doorstep, as in Nijmegen. "The civilian side of this war is in many ways the most pitiful," Gellhorn noted in the article "A Little Dutch Town," "they are ignorant of all the techniques soldiers learn; it takes a while to gauge shell bursts and to know what is dangerous and what is not."[47] In the meantime, the children stayed in cellars hoping for safety. Other less fortunate children lay in cellar hospitals with little food and no toys or distractions, just pain and displacement, loneliness and fear.

"A Little Dutch Town" also touched on a thread that runs throughout Gellhorn's writing—the documentation of atrocities committed by the Nazis. In the article, the issue of deportation arises and Gellhorn has glowing praise for the way the Dutch behaved in the face of the SS. With the strong revisionist undertones that threaten to taint our historical viewpoint, it was an appropriate time look again at pieces of primary documentation from all sources available, especially those which made into the public realm prior to the liberation and confirm the extent of the crimes committed against humanity.

Earlier in the March of 1944, Gellhorn wrote of the experiences of three Polish refugees she met in England.[48] The article documented details of the deportation of "300,000 people" from Silesia, mass executions, interrogations, systematic beatings and the Ghetto. She noted that "these men can testify to that life, and speak for the silenced millions."[49]

More painful details of atrocities are found in "Paris Revisited" and "Dachau." The pieces contain a parallel resonance which can become a little monotonous when the two are read in close succession, which is possibly why Gellhorn omitted "Paris Revisited" from the 1988 edition of *The Face of War*. However, both are important documentation of the legacy of the Third Reich.

"Paris Revisited" illustrated both German ingenuity and the fact that a city does not have to be bombed to suffer; torture scars the soul, if not the streets. The German genius for the practical is demonstrated in a variety of torture mechanism – sometimes the small and simple, an electric cord and a metal cap, ice cold tubs of water or a cold catacomb cell to slow starvation, hypothermia and death; others more complex and macabre, like the large brick ovens into which was inserted a large wooden box, lined with metal containing a prisoner who would be slowly roasted, burned alive. In Martha's words,

> It would take quite a while to die in those closed metal-lined boxes. First your feet burned, and when in agony you tried to raise yourself you reached for red hot hooks. As you could not stand, you were forced to lean against the glowing side walls of the box. And after you had been burned enough you would be brought out, cared for, questioned and if recalcitrant, put back into the box...human beings could scream for pain and find no other human being who would release them from such torment.[50]

Throughout the piece, Gellhorn stresses that she is showing only a small portion of the horror that took place in Paris.

In comparison, "Das Deutches Volk," Gellhorn went on to profile a miraculous German village with warehouses full of food -- chocolate, sugar, butter, almonds, candies and "more flour...than any of us had seen at one time."[51] By now Gellhorn was "all in temper, thinking of how well off the Germans had been" in this little village where none of the residents were Nazis. Of the village, she wrote:

> No one is a Nazi. No one ever was. There may have been some Nazi in the next village, as a matter of fact, that town about twenty kilometers away was a veritable hotbed of Nazidom...We were always known as very Red. Oh, the Jews? Well there weren't' really many Jews in this neighbor hood. Two maybe, maybe six. They were taken away. I hid a Jew for six weeks. I hid a Jew for eight weeks. (I hid a Jew, he hid a Jew, all God's Chillun hid Jews.)[52]

Gellhorn was angry and she did not hide her anger or personal feelings in the article. She had seen too much on the way to this village. She reminded the readers of a French village, Oradour, where the "Nazis locked every man, woman and child of the village into the church and set the church afire." This was in direct contrast to the German villagers who were weeping over furniture. She noted that "the Germans themselves have taught all the people of Europe not to waste time weeping over anything easy like furniture."[53]

In retrospect, Gellhorn's comments on the German village might seem a little harsh, but she was tired of Fascism. In her mind, she covered the period from the Spanish Civil War through to the end of World War II as one long war – a full nine years. Her dogged chase after the story and determination to cover the war took its toll. A letter to a *Collier's* editor written in early 1945 just after the Battle of the Bulge demonstrates her weary mental state:

> I must have a rest, by rest I probably mean escape, and I do not know whether I am simply tired to death or full of despair. There have been too many wars and they are all too long and finally one cannot endure it for other people. There

seems also to be a kind of selection backward, so that surely the bravest and the most innocent will be utterly destroyed.[54]

Gellhorn continued, echoing her youthful beliefs about the power of journalism:

> I am in despair about writing, too. I always thought that if I could make anyone who had not seen such suffering begin to imagine the suffering, they would insist on a world which refused to allow that suffering...I feel finally that the only thing I do with my writing is to give honor where honor is due, as if one carved a small, shabby, completely perishable monument for people who will get no other monument and will be, in any case, forgotten.[55]

It was a tough life. And there would be no rest, with the worst yet to come.

Gellhorn's article on the liberation of Dachau was one of the most powerful pieces of prose she wrote in her lifetime. If any one article encompasses the gist of Gellhorn's compassion and perception of the human condition, it is "Dachau." She brought home to the American public the reality of what happened at Dachau and the people that it happened to. From the experimentations to the solitary confinement chambers, to the crematorium, in "Dachau" she wrote:

> We have all seen a great deal now; we have seen too many wars and too much violent dying; we have seen hospitals, bloody and messy as butcher shops; we have seen the dead like bundles lying on all the roads of half the earth. But nowhere was there anything like this. Nothing about war was ever as insanely wicked as these starved and outraged, naked nameless dead. Be hind one pile of dead lay the

clothed healthy bodies of the German soldiers who had been found in this camp... And for the first time anywhere one could look at a dead man with gladness.[56]

With further observation, Martha continued:

> The women who were moved to Dachau three weeks ago from their own concentration camps. Their crime was that they were Jewish. There was a lovely girl from Budapest, who was somehow still lovely, and the woman with mad eyes who had watched her sister walk into the gas chamber at Auschwitz and been held back and refused the right to die with her sister...the day the American Army arrived...There were those who died cheering, because the effort of happiness was more than their bodies could endure. There were those who died because...they ate before they could be stopped, and it killed them. I do not know words to describe men who have survived this horror for years...and whose minds are as clear and unafraid as the day they entered.[57]

Martha Gellhorn was at Dachau when she heard the news of the German surrender and Dachau was to her "the most suitable place in Europe to hear the news of victory. For surely war was made to abolish Dachau, and all other places like Dachau, and everything that Dachau stood for, and to abolish it forever."[58]

World War II did not abolish war or concentration camps, or greed or arrogance or any other evil in mankind. In spite of her unique access to the Oval Office, Martha Gellhorn's journalistic efforts to show people the wrongs of the world so they could right them, did not work, any more than the newsreel footage of bombed cities and decaying bodies. Her writing, no matter how good, did not stop atrocities. She could not bring back the millions of dead. There was no "guiding light" of journalism to affect change.[59] Her career from Spain to Dachau proved that.

Later in life, she noted that the most important role journalists could play was to simply keep the record. In an interview from the 1990s, she was firm in her statement:

> It must be some place on the record because otherwise they can get by with anything. Does it stop anything? I have no feeling anything I've done has been of any use, but at least it is better than silence, because if you are silent, they can rewrite it anyway they want. They can make it look great, afterwards. So there is a point in it.[60]

What Gellhorn settled upon as her legacy from World War II was that of the role of witness.

---

[1] Amy Porter, "The Week's Work," *Collier's*, 4 March 1944, 43.

[2] Jenni Murray, "Martha Gellhorn: Her Views on Objective Reporting," in *Women's Hour* (BBC Radio 4, 7 April 1993).

[3] Ibid.

[4] Moorehead, *Gellhorn: A Twentieth-Century Life*, 207.

[5] The average reader of *Collier's* knew that Martha Gellhorn was a war correspondent. *Collier's* readers were use to reading articles from war fronts by Gellhorn. Just as readers of *Life Magazine* were used to seeing Margaret Bourke-White's photographs on the pages of the magazine since its inception, Gellhorn was at home on the pages of *Collier's*. While women in these front line roles were not the norm, readers were certainly not astonished by their presence.

[6] Martha Gellhorn, "Three Poles," *Collier's*, 18 March 1944, 17.

[7] Martha Gellhorn, "Children are Soldiers, Too," *Collier's*, 4 March 1944, 21.

[8] Ibid.

[9] Hemingway was authorized to go on ship, but not allowed to go onto the beach during the Invasion. In spite of that, his article "Over and Back," in which he falsely claimed to have landed, made it into publication in early July before Gellhorn's, which appeared in August.

[10] Ernest Hemingway, "Voyage to Victory," *Collier's*, 22 July 1944.

[11] Knightley, 231.

[12] U.S. National Archives, SHAEF Public Relations Office D-Day Directives, Folder 000.7-1.

[13] Gellhorn, *The Face of War*, 86.

[14] McLoughlin, *Martha Gellhorn: The War Writer in the Field and in the Text*, 125.

[15] Barry Bingham Sr. was the step son of rail magnate Henry Flagler's widow. His father Col. Robert Worth Bingham used his wife's money to purchase *The Louisville Times* and the *Courier Journal*. Bingham Sr. returned from the war and continued to build the Bingham family media group. He stepped down as CEO in 1971 and died in 1988.

[16] Hugh A. Mulligan, "Reporters in D-Day Invasion Couldn't Get Their Stories Out," *The Evening News*, 27 May 1984, 12B. The timing of the quote and information given by Bingham are noteworthy. While Martha Gellhorn was well known by a small cadre of individuals in 1984, republication of *The Face of War* and several of her works of fiction had not taken place. There is no reason to think Bingham had Gellhorn's account of D-Day or the PROs in mind when he made these statements.

[17] Gellhorn, *The Face of War (1959)*, "The First Hospital Ship" 141-55 and "D-Plus One: The Prisoners," 34-40.

[18] Rollyson, *Nothing Ever Happens to the Brave*, 196-99.

[19] Gellhorn, *The Face of War (1959)*, 145.

[20] Ibid., 150.

[21] Ibid., 146.

[22] Ibid., 150.

[23] Ibid.

[24] Rollyson, *Nothing Ever Happens to the Brave*, 7.

[25] Gellhorn, *The Face of War* (1959), 153-54.

[26] *Ibid.*, 86.

[27] U.S. National Archives, Supreme Headquarters Allied Expeditionary Forces (SHAEF) Public Relations Office, Press Policies, Folders 000.74-4 & 000.7-1

[28] At the beginning of American involvement in Europe, there was a question about what to do with women wanting accreditation as war-correspondents. This did not become critical until the North Africa landing. The minor resolution of the problem which allowed a few women correspondents to cover North Africa would take major revision before the D-Day. Most notably, Margaret Bourke White was assigned to a hospital ship during the North Africa landing, the supposedly safe place for a woman correspondent. Her ship took a hit, was sunk and the passengers were relegated to a lifeboat. Margaret Bourke-White, *Portrait of Myself* (Boston, Mass.: G.K. Hall, 1985). The general rule of thumb which was settled upon was that women correspondents could go no closer to the front than women service members. Lee Miller's photographs of the women in surgical tents on the beaches at Normandy are excellent examples of how the system was supposed to work. Her photos, of the use of napalm at St. Malo which led to her brief incarceration, were the opposite of what the PROs wanted. Lee Miller and Antony Penrose, *Lee Miller's War: Photographer and Correspondent with the Allies in Europe, 1944-45*, 1st North American ed. (Boston: Little, Brown, 1992). U.S. National Archives, Supreme Headquarters Allied Expeditionary Forces (SHAEF) Public Relations Office, Press Policies, Folders 000.74-4 & 000.7-1.

[29] Acton, *Memoirs of an Aesthete, 1939-1969*.

[30] The pilot was a member of "the Guinea Pig Club" burn victims who were treated with experimental, ground breaking burn therapy and reconstructive surgery by Dr. Sir Archibald MacIndoe.

[31] Gellhorn, *The Face of War* (1959), 120.

[32] Ibid., 210.

[33] Martha Gellhorn, Virginia Cowles, and Sandra Whipple Spanier, *Love Goes to Press: A Comedy in Three Acts* (Lincoln: University of Nebraska Press, 1995). Gellhorn gave a copy of the play to me when I visited her in June 1995. She encouraged me to read it to get a glimpse of her from that period. She noted that Cowles had written her character, and she wrote Cowles'.

[34] Gellhorn, Cowles, and Spanier, *Love Goes to Press: A Comedy in Three Acts*, vii.

[35] Gellhorn, *The Face of War* (1959),125-133

[36] Ibid., 129.

[37] Ibid.

[38] Ibid., 130.

[39] Ibid., 132.

[40] Ibid., 156.

[41] Ibid., 159.

[42] Ibid., 86.

[43] Gellhorn's articles from Nimjigen to Dachau are written as she proceeds across Europe with Gavin and the 82nd Airborne Division. She publishes a thank you article after the war ended. See Martha Gellhorn, "82nd Airborne: Master of the Hot Spots," *Saturday Evening Post* 23 February 1946.

[44] For a more detailed, but fictional account of the Battle of the Bulge by Gellhorn, read her novel *Point of No Return* (originally published in 1948 as *The Wine of Astonishment*). Martha Gellhorn, *Point of No Return*,

Plume American Women Writers (New York, N.Y.: New American Library, 1989).

[45] Gellhorn, *The Face of War (1959)*, 193.

[46] Ibid., 224.

[47] Ibid., 188.

[48] Ibid., 95-101.

[49] Ibid., 101.

[50] Ibid., 180-81.

[51] Ibid.

[52] Ibid., 213.

[53] Ibid., 219.

[54] Amy Porter and Martha Gellhorn, "The Week's Work," *Collier's,* 3 February 1945, 73.

[55] Ibid.

[56] Gellhorn, *The Face of War (1988)*, 184-85.

[57] Ibid., 185.

[58] Ibid.

[59] Gellhorn, *The Face of War (1988)*, 1.

[60] *Marie Colvin on Martha Gellhorn.*

CHAPTER 9

THE POST WAR AND POSTSCRIPTS

A few months after VE Day, the Hiroshima and Nagasaki bombs abruptly marked the end of the Second World War. Even if the designation "The Good War" is debatable, one thing remains certain; the conflict that ended in 1945 was Martha Gellhorn's war. She was horrified at the seemingly never ending brutality uncovered in the reconquest of Hitler's Europe.

The German Master Race perpetrated some of the worst horrors the world had ever seen and in some way Gellhorn connected America's belated entry into the war with the horror perpetrated. Nothing could erase in her mind the evil that had taken shape. At the same time, nothing slowed her writing down, and it was the best writing of her career. After World War II life would never be as clear, and her literary production would never be as consistently good.

After 1945, Gellhorn never again had the same optimistic faith in the goodness of humanity or the salutary powers of writing, although she continued to write until her death in 1998. While it lasted, World War II inspired what comprised Gellhorn's very best writing, both journalism and fiction. Fifteen years after she embarked on her youthful journey to become a novelist and foreign correspondent, she had also become that rarity she referred to as "an unscathed tourist of wars."[1]

For Gellhorn to end World War II, she had to write a book about the war, get it out of her system and onto paper.[2] She also longed to write a book that could compete with the quality of Hemingway's work: *The Point of No Return/Wine of Astonishment* was that product. Even with the completion of the book, Dachau still loomed heavily in Gellhorn's psyche and it would, regardless of her attempt to write it away, for the rest of her life.

The Point of No Return is the story of GI Jacob Levy and his journey across the ETO as a soldier. Levy happens to be a Jew, which is a non-issue to him, but is an issue with others in his unit. While he is not overtly hazed, it is clear that the soldiers around him are made very uncomfortable by the fact he is a Jew. This could well have paralleled Gellhorn's St. Louis experiences with latent anti-Semitism as a child. Yes, she and her family had been excluded from some social activities, but the Gellhorn family dealt with it rationally and took it in stride. Gellhorn did not discuss her Jewish background. There was nothing to discuss.[3]

In the same way Gellhorn refused to be treated as a second class citizen or be limited by the fact that she was a woman, she made an intentional effort in the book to "write like a man."[4] Gellhorn took great pride in the fact that the characters were her best and most believable. The novel is filled with insightful angst and internal dialogue. She was also pleased when she was complimented on her ability to write about battles and the battle field. The sights, smells and sounds she had stored away from her front line experiences and her journey across the continent with the 82nd Airborne were unpacked and spread thickly and effectively across the pages. Jacob Levy's journey culminated at Dachau. It was his breaking point, his point of no return.

From her earliest conceptualization of the book, Gellhorn knew the title: *The Point of No Return.* It was a reference to the aviation phrase meaning the point in a mission where there is no longer the opportunity to turn around and abort the mission. The point where there is no choice but to continue regardless of the circumstances. Gellhorn was talked out of the title by Max Perkins, her editor at Scribner's. Years later in 1988 when the book came back in to print, she gave it back its original title. For her reclaiming the title, was reclaiming her book. Clearly, World War II was Gellhorn's *Point of No Return*. Nothing in her life was ever the same.

Ironically, the original title *The Wine of Astonishment* also fit the book well, and in many ways it could also be applied to her immediate post war mood. Gellhorn chose the original title *The Wine of Astonishment* from Psalm 60: 3 The King James Version of the Bible:

> *O God, thou hast cast us off,*
> *Though hast scattered us,*
> *Though has been displeased;*
> *O turn thyself to us again.*
>
> *Thou hast made the earth to tremble;*
> *Though hast broken it;*
> *Heal the breaches thereof; for it shaketh*
> *Thou hast shewed thy people hard things:*
> *Thou hast made us to drink the wine of astonishment.*[5]

The Psalm is a psalm of urgent prayer requesting the restored favor of God, a request to set things right again. Ironically anyone picking up current most popular version of the *Holy Bible*, the *New International Version* (NIV), would not be able to find Gellhorn's reference. Gellhorn abandoned her *Wine of Astonishment* title, much as the *NIV* abandoned the reference.

The book was completed and so was the most dynamic period of Gellhorn's life. The period she was at her most prolific and productive was over. Nothing in her life came close to comparing or equaling her passion for Spain and no war, nor would anything else in her life be as clearly black and white as World War II. The fiction she produced was the best of her career. Her non-fiction of the period was her best writing and still provides readers with some of the best documentary literature of the 15 years between 1933 and 1948.

The latter phase of her life was marked by efforts at fiction which fell short of the mark of her other works. Her journalism was spotty and sporadic and often just a way to pay the bills or a vehicle for Gellhorn to see for herself what was happening in the world. No longer would she be closely attached to soldiers as she was to The Abraham Lincoln Brigade, or the Carpathian Lancers or the 82nd Airborne. She truly became an "unscathed tourist of wars."[6]

Gellhorn chose not to cover the Korean War. She ensconced herself into private life primarily in Cuernavaca, Mexico. She adopted an Italian war orphan, Sandy and they retreated from the outside world. She no longer had a home at *Collier's* to guarantee publication of her articles or income. While she was never fixed for an income, in Mexico she wrote formulaic stories and settled into a rhythm of life as a mother. She paid the bills and had enough income to rent a house and pay servants, and mixed with the likes of the Leonard Bernstein's and Gustav Reglar.

Gellhorn's relationship with her son was the most complex, tumultuous, and one of the longest in her life. Everything Gellhorn thought she knew about parenting came from her own parents. The stability of sheltered nurturing childhood, like the one provided by her father and supported by her mother, was the recipe she knew for parenting. Follow the recipe and the same result will logically follow. However, nurture vs. nature took sides and battled in Gellhorn's relationship with Sandy. He fell short often, due to fussiness early on, his weight battles throughout his youth and adulthood and later drug abuse and subsequent treatment. There is no doubt that the relationship miffed Gellhorn regularly, but she was in her own way always caring and supportive toward Sandy. No doubt she tried to follow the pattern set by Edna. He truly was her great personal challenge. A man she could not separate herself from, but one she loved deeply and was linked to as only a parent can be. She dedicated her finest book to him, *The Face of War*.

In 1959, after a decade of hit or miss writing, Gellhorn published her most important book, *The Face of War*. This was a gathering of the best of the best of her war reportage. The structure of the book was broken down into four sections: *The War in Spain*, *The War in Finland*, *The War in China* and *The Second World War*. Using the format of the book as a springboard for her personal commentary, in just under 25 printed pages, Gellhorn clearly defines herself as a writer and establishes the framework for the way we view her today.

The articles Gellhorn chose to reprint in the compilations of her work have served to shape the public's view of Gellhorn the journalist, Gellhorn the war correspondent, Gellhorn the liberal activist. While her selection as to what to include in her own edited versions of her articles are critical, her omissions are equally important. Her mundane articles, like the first novel she obliterated from any lists she made of her work, speak to the Martha Gellhorn who was developing her style and voice. They reflected the Martha Gellhorn who had not reached her apex of her career as a war reporter during the last year of World War II.

The articles she includes are her very best, and in the process of putting the book together, she took the liberty of polishing them and adding half a paragraph to her key article on Dachau. She notes on the final page of the book that she "tidied it a bit…I cut…" cleaning up the text. She describes it as just "the lightest quickest first aid job."[7] While Gellhorn was not heavy handed with her editing, she polished a little more than she hints at. For a general overview of the differences, the Collier's Collection at the New York Public Library is informative. However, Kate McLoughlin's textual analysis has the best comparison of Gellhorn's text from her notes, to the radioed transmissions, through the editors and onto the page.[8] The final published products in *The Face of War* are presented in exactly the manner Gellhorn wanted.

First and foremost, this was Gellhorn's book. It was completely separate from Hemingway. While later in *Travels with Myself and Another*, Gellhorn will write about her journey to China with Hemingway using the veiled UC (Unwilling Companion) instead of his name. In *The Face of War*, Hemingway is referenced only as "my journalist friend" in Spain.[9] He becomes the "we" in discussion of the journey through China. She references the period she made her final visit to Cuba to see Hemingway in the sentence: "From November 1943, with one unavoidable break in the spring of 1944, I followed the war wherever I could reach it."[10] The tone was set, and she continued to take the high road in nearly all matters published about Hemingway.

In the editorial sections, Gellhorn is in full correspondent voice. She is clear, deliberate, focused and in the mode to instruct and educate the reader. She noted:

> Journalism at its best and most effective is education....Journalism is a means; and I now think that the act of keeping the record straight is valuable in itself. Serious, careful, honest journalism is essential, not because it is a guiding light, but because it is a form of honorable behavior involving the reporter and the reader.[11]

It is a point of view that is in line closely with Theodore Roosevelt's 1906 Muckrake Speech. Later in subsequent interviews, Gellhorn kept repeating the idea of keeping the record straight, or as she often added being a "witness."[12]

After all the idealism, rhetoric, fighting the good fight, and winning the war, the 1939-45 war did not make the world safe for democracy, any more than World War I had. This was acutely so in Eastern Europe where Nazi tyranny only gave way to decades of Communist oppression, totalitarianism and despotism. Yalta and Potsdam set the stage for forty years of superpower confrontation in the Cold War and the reverberations from Hiroshima and Nagasaki served as a permanent reminder of the nightmare possibility of nuclear annihilation. Change and progress, which she had such faith in as a youth, became the agent of uncertainty and disillusion. In *The Face of War* she is clear about her concerns and her hope that "memory and imagination, not nuclear weapons, are the great deterrents."[13]

Gellhorn's deftness with words is attested to by the fact that she was able to stake out the most crucial themes in her work by reprinting 20 articles and writing less than a total of 25 printed pages of commentary. In those fewer than 25 total printed pages, Gellhorn took control of her legacy in the most constructive and powerful way she knew possible, in her own words.

Twenty years after the end of World War II and thirty years after Spain, she returned to a war zone. Vietnam was a war like nothing she had witnessed before; Vietnam was a war like the US had never fought before. She had no way to know what a transformative experience her short time in Vietnam would be.

Martha Gellhorn was no longer a war correspondent and as with Spain, she had to use her connections and reputation to get in to the country, and then paid her own airfare to get to Saigon.[14] She was no Dickie Chapelle on the frontline, trudging through the jungle attached to the Marine Corps and covering the war from the front. She no longer had an affiliation and pay from a magazine like *Collier's*. It was a new kind of war and a new kind of war correspondent's role for Gellhorn. From Spain, she meandered the war fronts through World War II and her articles reached a millions of readers. This time, her articles again focused on people, but were not written from the front. They also did not have a potential audience of millions. Circumstances had changed, but Gellhorn's clear eye had not. She still saw what was happening in the streets and in the faces of the people of Vietnam and it was not good. She was so impassioned she produced a half a dozen articles from the few weeks she was there.

The articles she were published in small circulation media, *The Guardian*, a Catholic magazine, and Gellhorn's still steady fallback *The St. Louis Post Dispatch*. But, the tone and topic and overall spirit of Gellhorn's articles were enough to incense the State Department, and Gellhorn was one of three journalist banned from reentry to South Vietnam.[15]

Gellhorn went on to cover the Six Day War and visit Central America during the early 1980s. Another edition of *The Face of War* was reprinted in 1988. While several powerful articles are lost, they are replaced them with sections on Vietnam and the wars in Central America, adding breadth to her legacy, and bringing her journalism to a younger audience. There is more bite to her commentary, especially in regard to Ronald Reagan and Margaret Thatcher.

After her return from Vietnam in 1966, she ran in to diplomat George Kennan. The meeting sparked a long correspondence between the two and Gellhorn vented her political passion to him. They had met briefly in Prague during the Czech crisis and Kennan had not been impressed with her, summing her up as another "ill-informed do-gooder." In Prague, Kennan did not foresee she was to become an influential war correspondent. In her letters to others, her attempt to hold on to her position as a writer of importance is clear. To her friend from Spain, Alvah Bessie she wrote:

> If I had a fine memory (one of the basic ingredients of talent), I might be able to write Memoirs, better than George Kennan for instance because, from my worms eye view, I do believe I saw the world more truly.[16]

She truly believed she saw politics and the world more clearly than others.

Gellhorn's egotistical assertion of her more accurate "worm's eye" view was contradicted by her often black and white stances on political issues. Gellhorn was not perfect and at times keenly demonstrated a lack of situational awareness and understanding of her surroundings. An article published on Cuba in the 1980s and included in *The View from the Ground* demonstrated this flaw in awareness. She noted that in Cuba:

> A delightful little black kid bounced out of somewhere, in spotless white shirt and royal blue shorts. He smiled up at me with a look of true love and undying trust. "Rusa?" he asked. I was mortally offended. Russian women of certain age, seen in Moscow, had bodies like tanks and legs like tree trunks.[17]

Gellhorn often protested that she had not traded on her looks in her youth, but at nearly 80 years old, Gellhorn was offended over a slight regarding her looks. Even more telling was her assessment of

Cuba when she lived there in the late 1930s and early 1940s. She wrote:

> In my time, no one ever talked politics or bothered to notice which gang was in office and robbing the till. I cannot remember any elections...One day driving in to Havana, I heard shooting and Solomon or the street boys advised me to settle in the Floridita and drink frozen daiquiris until it was over..."[18]

This was during a time which Gellhorn resided primarily in Cuba. The woman who was supposed to have her finger on the pulse of the people was surrounded by the people and living conditions which bred the Cuban Revolution of 1959 and she didn't even notice. To further demonstrate her lack of situational awareness, she admitted that "I had never thought of Cubans as blacks"[19] The woman who was a perpetual traveler noted that "I had never bothered to travel in Cuba when I lived here, and had no sense of its size or of the variety of towns and the landscape."[20]

The View From The Ground acts as a compliment to *The Face of War*. Published in 1988, it included what Gellhorn considered the best of her non-war reporting. It is constructed like *The Face of War*, but instead of the sections being divided by wars, each section of reportage is divided into decades from the 1930s to the 1980s. Again, as with *The Face of War*, Gellhorn uses the opportunity to inserts her commentary at the end of each decade's articles. In many ways, *The View From the Ground* serves as a bookend to *The Face of War*. In *The Face of War*, Gellhorn sets out the cornerstones of her legacy. *The View From the Ground* just compliments that and reinforces the ideals Gellhorn wants to leave her readers and posterity with. While it is not the last thing she wrote, in many ways it reinforced what she wanted to be her last word.

---

[1] The Face of War (1959), 88.

[2] John Pilger, "The Outsiders: Martha Gellhorn."

[3] It was not until Milton Wolff read Carl Rollyson's biography of Gellhorn, *Nothing Ever Happens to the Brave*, that he became aware of her Jewish heritage.

[4] Gellhorn, *Point of No Return*, 328.

[5] The only version of Psalm 60:1-3 that has the phrase "wine of astonishment" is the traditional King James Version of the Bible. The alternative Bible placed in motels is the Gideon's New King James Version (the Modern English –MEV) Psalm 60:3 uses the phrase "the wine of confusion." The currently most popular translation the New International Version of the Bible also uses the phrase "wine that makes us stagger." The irony is that if a modern reader were to read the Psalm, they probably would find the quote and find it difficult to see the proper reference and read it in the context of the Psalm. To the modern reader The Wine of Astonishment as a title was equivocally abandoned by Gellhorn.

[6] Gellhorn, *The Face of War* (1988), 16.

[7] Gellhorn, *The Face of War* (1959), 245.

[8] McLoughlin, *Martha Gellhorn: The War Writer in the Field and in the Text*.

[9] Gellhorn, *The Face of War* (1959), 12.

[10] Ibid., 108.

[11] Ibid., 3-4.

[12] See Murray, *Martha Gellhorn: Her Views on Objective Reporting*, *Marie Colvin on Martha Gellhorn*, or John Pilger, *The Outsiders: Martha Gellhorn*. Gellhorn used available opportunities to drive home this point.

[13] Gellhorn, *The Face of War* (1959), 8.

[14] *Marie Colvin on Martha Gellhorn.*

[15] Knightley, 442.

[16] Gellhorn and Moorehead, *The Collected Letters of Martha Gellhorn,* 955.

[17] Gellhorn, *The View from the Ground, 381.*

[18] Ibid., 392.

[19] Ibid., 386.

[20] Ibid., 391.

EPILOGUE

By the turn of the 21st Century, Gellhorn had effectively lost the anchor of the Hemingway legacy and emerged from his shadow fully, as a writer on her own merits In her career, she did not rise to his level as a novelist, but she far exceeded him as a journalist. What is clear is that in the 1980s and 1990s, the woman Hemingway's vilified as a "cold hearted bitch ('s)" time had come. She had outlasted Hemingway by 35 years and began the process of reclaiming that portion of her life by writing *Travels with Myself and Another*.[1]

In the last decades of her life, Gellhorn occasionally and sparingly appeared on the video screen and in radio interviews and her voice matched the tone and cadence of her best journalism. That voice was the same one she used on paper in the biographical tidbits she wrote for *The Face of War*, *The View From the Ground* and the *Afterwords* of the novels which were republished in the 1980s and 1990s. It is very much the solid and sage voice of "Martha Gellhorn." It is that Martha Gellhorn who is a role model for an entirely new generation of young women. A symbol of feminism who powerfully transcends feminism. She is the woman men admire and young women want to be like.

Gellhorn will continue to fascinate and future scholarly work will shed more and more light on her legacy. Her papers will open up and we will be able to read the rest of the letters, the notes, diaries and stillborn books; the papers Gellhorn intentionally left for us to read.

In the meantime, the bits and pieces, truths and mistruths, myths and hyperbole and come together to formed a mosaic of Martha Gellhorn. And, to a certain extent, that image has taken on a life of its own. The single document which encapsulates and demonstrates the most current reflection of "Martha Gellhorn" best is Marie Colvin's BBC portrait of Gellhorn. Released just before Colvin's death in February 2012, in 4 minutes it boils down the essence of the present myth of Gellhorn. "The first...the best...the only...the woman who...the most objective..."[2] Those same themes are echoed in nearly all the available BBC archival materials and much of what has been written about Gellhorn after her death. But, Martha Gellhorn was not the first woman war correspondent, nor was she the only woman on the scene. Her status as the "best" war correspondent is debatable.

What is clear is that from the beginning of her career, Gellhorn's desire was to honestly explain, to educate and to hope for a resultant change for the better. This was first and foremost. The change did not come, in spite of her access to powerful policy makers and a massive reading audience. She noted, "It took nine years, and a great depression and two wars ending in defeat to break my faith in the benign power of the press."[3]

Later in life, Gellhorn settled on what she believed to be the longer lasting legacy of her work and reportage. Her work served to bear witness to what had happened. She noted that "journalism at its best and most effective is education."[4] In her mind, witnesses educate and keep the story straight and guard against both nostalgic and sinister revisionism.

Witnesses are the sentinels who keep watch over history and stand in the way of those who would try to alter, soften, reframe and apologize for the atrocities of the times. It is in that most important role, Gellhorn continues to teach, enlighten and illuminate readers.

---

[1] Martha Gellhorn, *Travels With Myself And Another* (London: Allen Lane, 1978); Gellhorn Interview, 14 June 1995.

[2] *Marie Colvin on Martha Gellhorn.*

[3] The Face of War (1988), p. 1.

[4] Ibid, p. 3.

SELECTED BIBLIOGRAPHY

Abshire, Mary. "Psychiana." http://www.class.uidaho.edu/narrative/theory/psychiana.htm. n.d. Web accessed 10 September 2010.

Acton, Harold. *Memoirs of an Aesthete, 1939-1969*. New York: Viking Press, 1971.

Anderson, Brian C. "Bertrand De Jouvenel's Melancholy Liberalism." *Public Interest*, No. 143 (2001): 87.

Arnold, Lloyd R. *High on the Wild with Hemingway*. Caxton Printers, 1968.

Baker, Carlos. *Ernest Hemingway: A Life Story*. New York: Scribner, 1969.

_____. *Carlos Baker Collection of Ernest Hemingway*. Princeton University Library Manuscripts Division: Princeton New Jersey.

Bauman, John F. and Thomas H. Coode. *In the Eye of the Great Depression: New Deal Reporters and the Agony of the American People*. DeKalb: Northern Illinois University Press, 1988.

Blair, Emily Newell, and Virginia Jeans Laas. *Bridging Two Eras: The Autobiography of Emily Newell Blair, 1877-1951*. Columbia: University of Missouri Press, 1999.

Blair, Lawrence. *Survey Graphic* (December 1936): 684.

Bloom, Harold. *Upton Sinclair's the Jungle*, Chelsea House Publishers, 2002.

Bourke-White, Margaret. *Portrait of Myself*. Boston, Mass.: G.K. Hall, 1985.

"Bryn Mawr Women as Suffragists: The Nawsa Alumnae." http://www.brynmawr.edu/library/exhibits/suffrage/nawsaAl ums.html#tableau. Bryn Mawr Library Special Collections. n.d. Web accessed 14 April 2012:

Burke, Carolyn. *Lee Miller: A Life.* New York: Knopf, 2005.

Colvin, Marie. "Marie Colvin on Martha Gellhorn -- the First Female War Correspondent." BBC/Daily Motion, http://www.dailymotion.com/video/xoyt82_marie-colvin-on-martha-gellhorn-the-first-female-war-reporter_shortfilms. 2012. February 2012. Web accessed 15 April 2012.

Cook, Blanche Wiesen. *Eleanor Roosevelt,* Viking, 1992.

Corbett, Katharine T. *In Her Place: A Guide to St. Louis Women's History.* St. Louis: Missouri Historical Society Press, 1999.

Cowles, Virginia. *Looking for Trouble.* New York: Harper Brothers, 1941.

Crane, Richard Francis. "A French Conscience in Prague: Louis Eugene Faucher and the Abandonment of Czechoslovakia." Boulder, CO.: Columbia University Press, 1996.

"Czechoslovakia." *Life Magazine,* 30 May 1938, 50-64.

Dorman, Angelia. "Telephone Interview with Martha Gellhorn." 28 February 1990.

_____. "Interview with Jack Hemingway." Sun Valley, ID 15 August 1992.

_____. "Telephone Interview with Tillie Arnold." 22 August 1992.

_____. "Interview with Martha Gellhorn." London, 21 June 1995.

_____. "Interview with Martha Gellhorn." London, 11 August 1991.

_____. "Interview with Martha Gellhorn." London, 14 June 1995.

_____. "Interview with Milton Wolff." El Cerrito, CA. 20-26 August 1999.

_____. "Interview with Elizabeth McIntosh." Woodbridge VA. 17-18 August 2009.

Eby, Carl P. *Hemingway's Fetishism: Psychoanalysis and the Mirror of Manhood*. SUNY Series in Psychoanalysis and Culture. Albany: State University of New York Press, 1999.

"Edna Gellhorn." Experiencing Women's History in Missouri, http://missouriwomen.org/2010/10/24/edna-gellhorn/.n.d. Web 10 April 2012.

Elizabeth, McDonald (McIntosh). "Hemingways Answer Call to Adventure." Honolulu Star Bulletin, 5 February 1941.

Forde, Nigel. "Martha Gellhorn: Democracy, Power, and President Roosevelt." *Bookshelf*. BBC Radio 4, 4 January 1990.

_____. "Martha Gellhorn: The Difference between Fiction and Reporting." *Bookshelf*. BBC Radio 4, 4 January 1990.

_____. Martha Gellhorn "The Spanish Civil War." *Bookshelf*. BBC Radio 4, 4 January 1990.

"Four Panels Illustrate Martha Gellhorn's Theme." *The New York Times*, 27 September 1936, 3.

Gellhorn, Martha. "82nd Airborne: Master of the Hot Spots." *Saturday Evening Post*, 23 February 1946, 22-23ff.

_____. "A Little Worse Than Peace." *Collier's*, 14 November 1942.

_____. *A Stricken Field*, Virago Modern Classics. London: Penguin Books: Virago Press, 1986.

_____. "Children Are Soldiers, Too." *Collier's*, 4 March 1944.

_____. "Come Ahead, Adolf!" *Collier's*, 6 August 1938.

_____. "Correspondence with Angelia Dorman." 19 May 1989-9 January 1998.

_____. "Correspondence with Eleanor Roosevelt." edited by Eleanor Roosevelt. Hyde Park, New York: Franklin D. Roosevelt Library.

_____. "Correspondence with Ernest Hemingway." Boston: Ernest Hemingway Collection, John F. Kennedy Library.

_____. "Geneva Portraits." *St. Louis Post Dispatch*, 20 November 1930, 2D.

_____. "Holland's Last Stand." 25-27: Collier's, 26 December 1942.

_____. *Liana*, Virago Modern Classics. New York: NY, Penguin Books-Virago Press, 1987.

_____. *Liana*. New York: C. Scribner's Sons, 1944.

_____. "Men without Medals." *Collier's*, 15 January 1938, 49.

_____. "Notations on *a Critical Biography of Martha Gellhorn* by Jacqueline Elizabeth Orsagh." 1989.

_____. "Obituary of a Democracy." *Collier's*, 10 December 1938.

_____. "On Apocryphsm." *The Paris Review*, Spring, 1981.

_____. *Point of No Return*, Plume American Women Writers. New York: NY, New American Library, 1989.

_____. *Pretty Tales for Tired People*. New York: Simon and Schuster, 1965.

_____. "Singapore Scenario." *Collier's*, 9 August 1941, 20-21, 43-44.

_____. *The Face of War*. New York: Atlantic Monthly Press, 1988.

_____. *The Face of War*. New York: Simon and Schuster, 1959.

_____. *The Heart of Another*. New York: Scribner's, 1941.

_____. *The Novellas of Martha Gellhorn*. 1st American ed. New York: Knopf, 1993.

_____. *The Trouble I've Seen*. New York: W. Morrow and company, 1936.

_____. *The View from the Ground*. New York: Atlantic Monthly Press, 1988.

_____. *Travels with Myself and Another*. London: Allen Lane, 1978.

_____. *Travels with Myself and Another*. New York: Putnam, 2001.

_____. "Three Poles." *Collier's*, 18 March 1944, 17.

_____. "Writers Fighting in Spain." Paper presented at the 2nd American Writers' Congress, New York, 1937.

Gellhorn, Martha, Virginia Cowles, and Sandra Whipple Spanier. *Love Goes to Press: A Comedy in Three Acts*. Lincoln: University of Nebraska Press, 1995.

Gellhorn, Martha, and Caroline Moorehead. *The Collected Letters of Martha Gellhorn*. 1st ed. New York: H. Holt, 2006.

Grattan, C. Hartley. "Behind the Figures." *The New Republic* (21 October 1936): 328.

Graves, Karen. *Girls' Schooling During the Progressive Era: From Female Scholar to Domesticated Citizen*. Garland Reference Library of Social Science, New York: Garland Pub., 1998.

Greene, Graham. "Review of *the Trouble I've Seen*." *Spectator* (22 May 1936): 950.

Hack, Karl and Kevin Blackburn. *Forgotten Captives in Japanese-Occupied Asia*. Routledge, 2008.

Harley, Don Edward. "Walter Gellhorn FBI File, File No. 101-603-2-43."

"He Was a Right Guy and the Woman with Him Was Good Looking: For the Hemingways There'll Be No Farewell to Arms." *San Francisco Chronicle*, 31 January 1940.

Hemingway, Ernest. *Across the River and into the Trees*. Scribner, 1950.

_____. "Voyage to Victory." *Collier's*, 22 July 1944.

Hofstadter, Richard. *The Age of Reform: From Bryan to F. D. R.* New York: Knopf, 1955.

Holsinger, M. Paul. *War and American Popular Culture: A Historical Encyclopedia*. Greenwood Press, 1999.

Hopkins, June. *Harry Hopkins: Sudden Hero, Brash Reformer*. The Franklin and Eleanor Roosevelt Institute Series on Diplomatic and Economic History. New York: St. Martin's Press, 1999.

Kerrane, Kevin, and Ben Yagoda. *The Art of Fact: A Historical Anthology of Literary Journalism*. New York, NY: Scribner, 1997.

Kert, Bernice. *The Hemingway Women*. W.W. Norton, 1998.

Knightley, P. *The First Casualty: The War Correspondent as Hero and Myth-Maker from the Crimea to Iraq*. Johns Hopkins University Press, 2004.

Lloyd, Gordon, Herbert Hoover, and Franklin D. Roosevelt. *The Two Faces of Liberalism: How the Hoover-Roosevelt Debate Shapes the 21st Century*. M&M Scrivener Press, 2006.

Lumpkin, Grace. *To Make My Bread*, The Radical Novel Reconsidered. Urbana: University of Illinois Press, 1995.

Lynn, Andrea. *Shadow Lovers: The Last Affairs of H.G. Wells*. Boulder: Westview Press, 2001.

"Martha Gellhorn, Reporter - Wife of Ernest Hemingway, Clippers into Town." *San Francisco Chronicle*, 28 May 1941, 28.

Matthews, Herbert L. *The Education of a Correspondent*. Harcourt, Brace and Company, 1946.

McLachlan, Sean. *It Happened in Missouri*. 1st ed, It Happened in Series. Guilford, Conn.: Globe Pequot Press, 2008.

McLoughlin, Kate. *Martha Gellhorn: The War Writer in the Field and in the Text*. Manchester University Press, 2007.

Meyers, Jeffrey. *Hemingway: A Biography*. Da Capo Press, 1999.

Miller, Lee, and Antony Penrose. *Lee Miller's War: Photographer and Correspondent with the Allies in Europe, 1944-45*. Boston: Little, Brown, 1992.

Mink, Gwendolyn. *The Wages of Motherhood: Inequality in the Welfare State, 1917-1942*. Ithaca, NY: Cornell University Press, 1995.

Moorehead, Caroline. *Gellhorn: A Twentieth-Century Life*. New York: Henry Holt, 2003.

Moreira, Peter. *Hemingway on the China Front: His WWII Spy Mission with Martha Gellhorn*. 1st ed. Washington, DC: Potomac Books, Inc., 2005.

Mort, T.A. *The Hemingway Patrols: Ernest Hemingway and His Hunt for U-Boats*. New York: Scribner, 2009.

Mulligan, Hugh A. "Reporters in D-Day Invasion Couldn't Get Their Stories Out." *The Evening News*, 27 May 1984, 12B.

Murray, Jenni. "Martha Gellhorn: Her Views on 'Objective' Reporting. W*omen's Hour*, BBC Radio 4, 7 April 1993.

_____. "Martha Gellhorn: Where Her Confidence Comes From." W*omen's Hour*, BBC Radio 4, 7 April 1993.

O'Sullivan, Noel. *Political Theory in Transition*. London ; New York: Routledge, 2000.

Orsagh, Jacqueline Elizabeth. *A Critical Biography of Martha Gellhorn.* Michigan State University, 1978.

_____. "Discussions between Orsagh and Dorman." October 1988-April 2012.

Ostroff, Roberta. *Fire in the Wind: The Life of Dickey Chapelle.* New York: Ballantine Books, 1992.

Porter, Amy, and Martha Gellhorn. "The Week's Work." *Collier's,* 3 February 1945, 73.

Pilger, John. "The Outsiders: Martha Gellhorn." A Tempest Films Production for Channel Four 1983. http://www.youtube.com/watch?v=GDFOZQzByfw. 1983. Web 2 February 2012.

Rabe, Robert A. "Marquis W. Childs." In *Encyclopedia of American Journalism,* edited by Stephen Vaughn, 95-96. New York: Routledge, 2008.

Rollyson, Carl E. *Beautiful Exile: The Life of Martha Gellhorn.* London: Aurum Press, 2001.

_____. *Nothing Ever Happens to the Brave: The Story of Martha Gellhorn.* 1st ed. New York: St. Martin's, 1990.

Roosevelt, Theodore. "The Man with the Muck-Rake." American Rhetoric.com, http://www.americanrhetoric.com/speeches/teddyrooseveltm uckrake.htm. n.d. Web accessed 1 April 2012.

Scott, A. O. "When We Read Red." *Nation* 263, No. 8 (1996): 30-32.

Shakespeare, Nicholas. "Martha Gellhorn." *Granta* 62, Summer (1998): 216-35.

"Speaking of Pictures." *Life,* January 15, 1948, 8, 9, 11.

"The Coeur D'Alene Press." Coeur D'Alene Idaho, 25 July-28 November, 1935.

Thomas, Hugh. *The Spanish Civil War*. New York: Harper & Row, 1986.

Thompson, Nichols. "The Hawk and the Dove: Paul Nitze, George Kennan, and the History of the Cold War." New York: Henry Holt and Company, 2009.

van Doren, Dorothy. "Shorter Notices." *Nation,* 143, No. 18 (1936): 528-29.

Watson, William Branch. "The Hemingway Review." *Spanish Civil War Issue* VII, No. 2, no. Spring, 1988.

Wiebe, Robert H. *The Search for Order, 1877-1920*. Westport, Conn.: Greenwood Press, 1980.

Williams, Emily. "Oral History Interview: Martha Gellhorn." St. Moritz Hotel: Franklin Delano Roosevelt Library, 20 February 1980.

Willis, Jim. *100 Media Moments That Changed America*. Santa Barbara, Calif.: Greenwood Press, 2010.

Wiser, W. *The Twilight Years: Paris in the 1930s*. Robson Books, 2001.

Wrightstone, J.W. *Appraisal of Experimental High School Practices*: Teachers College, Columbia University, 1936.

Wyden, Peter. The Passionate War: The Narrative History of the Spanish Civil War, 1936-1939. New York: Simon and Schuster, 1983.

ABOUT THE AUTHOR

Angelia Hardy Dorman earned her BA and MAT in History from the
University of South Carolina and a Ph.D. in History from the University of
Idaho. Originally from Berkeley County, South Carolina, she currently
resides with her husband and two children in Central Washington State.
Her interest in Gellhorn began in 1987 when she first read Gellhorn's work
at the Berkeley County Public Library.
She can be contacted by email: angiedorman@gmail.com

Lightning Source UK Ltd.
Milton Keynes UK
UKOW041834181212

203853UK00001B/92/P